A Different Woman
The View from Ninety

A Different Woman
The View from Ninety

Essays by

JOAN KIP

CONFLUX PRESS · MARINA DEL REY

ISBN: 978-0-9861134-0-6

Cover painting: *Sky, Sea, Land* by Olivia Eielson
Author photo: Kip Family Archives
Cover & book design: Tania Baban-Natal

Printed in the United States of America

CONFLUX PRESS
Marina del Rey, California
www.confluxpress.com

For Art

Acknowledgements

The author wishes to thank the editors of the following magazines and anthologies where these essays first appeared, some in earlier versions or with different titles:

Bellevue Literary Review: "Bereavement and Beyond";
  "Solitude"; "The House Across from the Park"
Branches: "Mother and Daughter"
Dark Moon Lilith: "The Collector"
Driftwood: "Widowhood"
Rockhurst Review: "A Farewell"
Steam Ticket: "Paris"
Tiferet: "The Gentle Art of Dying"

"The House Across from the Park" was also nominated for a 2010 Pushcart Prize and received *Bellevue Literary Review*'s 2010 Carter V. Cooper Memorial Prize for Nonfiction, judged by Phillip Lopate. "A Different Woman" was included in *Still Going Strong: Memoirs, Stories, and Poems About Great Older Women* (Haworth Press, 2005). "Bereavement and Beyond" was reprinted in the *Bellevue Literary Review Anthology* (BLR, 2007).

Table of Contents

Introduction

I met Joan Kip in Berkeley, California in March of 1998 at the birthday party of a mutual friend. Joan was eighty years old; I was thirty-five. She had recently lost her husband, Art, to a heart attack. I had just met the man I would marry. Joan and I introduced ourselves at the buffet table that evening and soon began talking about writing, a conversation that would last the next fifteen years. Though Joan was grieving, she held herself with grace and dignity. She explained [to me] that she was sorry she had to leave the party early, but she was returning home to write to Art, something she'd done every night since his death. The letters Joan penned to Art would become the seeds of this book.

Soon after that party, Joan telephoned to ask if she could hire me as her editor. We met for lunch the following week in her dining room that opened on to the garden Art had designed. It was in this airy space that we would meet hundreds of times over the next decade and a half, to read and discuss the essays Joan crafted from the depths of her soul. Joan made soup and served pizza from The Cheeseboard, poured us each a glass of wine, and settled in to discuss all matters of the heart and aging—love and sex and friendship—and, of course, the craft of writing.

Extremely well read and erudite, Joan had a keen and inquiring mind, a huge vocabulary, and a wise and determined heart. She worked with a focused perseverance and continued to send her writing into the world even after receiving those inevitable first rejection letters. She never let go of her dream to see her work published. She would instead return to her desk to re-write her essays until she felt she had gotten what she wanted to say exactly right. Within several years, her letters to Art had coalesced into a small collection of essays that were finding homes in newspapers, anthologies, and literary magazines.

During the years we worked together, typed letters arrived in my mailbox monthly, accompanied with drafts of Joan's latest essays, each containing a yellow post-it note that instructed in no uncertain terms: "Karin"—with her British accent Joan always called me Karin, something I adored—"Please find enclosed the last and final version. Here it is finished forever! Love, J." Months later, we'd laugh during a work session in Berkeley, both of us knowing all too well that there had been many more drafts of that same essay written.

One of Joan's earliest acceptances came from the *San Jose Mercury News*. I remember her standing on the deck above her garden, holding that newspaper with a shy pride. Those early publications served to feed her determination and strengthen her belief in herself and in her writing. Occasionally doubt sometimes crept back in, as it did when she called one morning to ask if a one-sentence mention in the *New York Times Arts Section* was good, and I had to explain that, yes, a one sentence mention in *that* publication was *very* good. Later, when Joan placed second in a literary competition, I thought I heard something more underneath her professed happiness. Probing deeper, she finally admitted that she had wanted first prize, not second. It was this spark of desire that moved Joan to write more honest and less varnished prose, to forever attempt to reveal her truest self, and to find exactly the right words for it all. This kind of writing takes a great deal of time, commitment, and courage to come to fruition, and Joan was all too aware that she was running out of time. She kept writing and re-writing, however. One publication she greatly admired was *The Bellevue Literary Review*. "I'm not sure my essays are ready yet, Karin," she said with a glint in her eye, though we both knew that she would write the perfect cover letter and submit her best efforts. Three of her submissions were accepted over the next few years and published in *BLR*. One of her essays was awarded first prize in a national contest judged by Phillip Lopate and nominated for a Pushcart Prize.

As a hospice counselor for many years, Joan wrote through the deaths of close friends and clients, through her experiment of taking a lover after Art had died, through her hip surgery and cancer treatments. She never stopped putting her life on the page and never settled for easy answers. She reached a place where she was fully and completely in service to her craft. She loved her friends and her family deeply, with great intensity and interest, with concern and respect; and she equally treasured her time alone with the page and her words and her heart. Telling her truth was paramount to Joan's existence. She would sit with her essays for days, weeks, months, incubating them, going over every word and reading them out loud to me at her dining room table, where sometimes she wept and sometimes she laughed, marveling at all that she had lived.

Writing brought Joan a tremendous joy and happiness. She was not afraid to re-examine the depths of her unfolding: surviving the bombs dropped on London during World War II, leaving England for an unknown country with a new husband, questioning whether she had been a good enough daughter, friend, mother, grandmother—and realizing herself as not only a devoted wife who had adored her husband for fifty-two years, but also a woman who embraced and celebrated the freedom she enjoyed after his death. The essays included in *A Different Woman: The View From Ninety* were written for all of us as we survive our losses, grow older, and meet our last days, too, on this beautiful blue and green planet.

Joan Kip was a rare true friend and trusted confidant until the end. I'm happy to say that she died knowing this collection of nineteen essays would be published and given to a wider audience. It was a pact we had made, sitting side by side with her typed pages between us. She loved imagining this book, and her delighted smile then was much like the smile I see in her author photograph. I am blessed to have been a small part of her journey and, along with her closest friends and family, deliver this collection of essays into your care.

Karen Benke
February 24, 2015
Mill Valley, California

3

The House Across from the Park

Time is a river, a violent current of events,
glimpsed once and already carried past us,
and another follows and is gone.

Marcus Aurelius

I open my eyes this still, foggy morning and peer at the clock on the wall opposite the bed—the clock that Art designed over fifty-seven years ago. A disk, painted white, with the hour and minute hands fashioned out of black electrician's tape, it was to be temporary. Like so many other projects around the house: our bed frame Art made from a plank of used plywood, the living room couch built out of secondhand pine, painted black to hide its knots, the dining room table carved out of a damaged door we brought to Berkeley from our first house in Massachusetts. Mementos from our days of frugality, retooled many times over, they remain brazen in their refusal to relocate to a receptive Salvation Army. Not yet ready to greet the day, I remain in the twilight zone of emerging consciousness, my mind drifting along its idle path until I am aware that I'm thinking of that dining room table—of the first time we met: each of us, in a way, damaged.

* * *

It had been a long and humid moving day as I drove along the Massachusetts Turnpike from Cambridge to our new home in Lexington. Art had preceded us, together with our furniture and Jonathan, our four-year-old son, whose exuberance was tempered by a chronic ear infection. My mother-in-law, Alice, squeezed alongside me in our packed, 1935 Ford, holding three-week-old Jennifer, who wailed inconsolably with hunger pains—rhythmic, echoing wailings that shred a mother's gut. Then, inexplicably, the car lights failed. Back in the forties there were few bright lights on the highways and, except for passing cars, one depended on the moon and stars and an assumed faith in the benignity of the gods. Off the highway and up the winding hill, aided by lights from neighborhood houses, I finally saw the light shining from our own carport, and Art, standing there in the driveway, unpacking boxes. Still recovering from the polio that had felled me some weeks earlier, I trembled with exhaustion and a pervasive guilt that my daughter would die from maternal neglect. But I was home now with a bathroom not yet connected to its plumbing, and a kitchen lonely for a stove. Art, whose energy was on automatic recharge, led me by the hand and pointing to a door balanced between two trestles in the middle of the living room, pronounced with biblical exactitude, "Look, the perfect table!" Sinking into a weathered chair, I caressed that pinewood door—an emblem of permanent solidity—as if it in some way reconnected me to the earth. There, surrounded by boxes, my feet on that accommodating door, I unbuttoned my blouse and nursed our daughter.

* * *

The telephone next to my bed jolts me awake. I pick up the phone and hear "Hi, Mum," as Jen's bouncy voice floats out to greet me from Guatemala. Fifty-nine years old, she lives in Panajachel, a predominantly Mayan pueblo along the shores of Lake Atitlan. We exchange daily, uncensored chats, sharing intimate and unprintable happenings in our lives. If I'm out, she calls Jon in Los

Angeles who, in turn, calls me. A family ring-a-round that invokes recollections of a yesteryear when this house was young and every room was occupied.

Alone without Art the house and I co-exist in a complicity of dependent love. Fifty years ago, friends stood on the deck off our living room, high up among the Redwood trees, and gazed across the park at the wonders of the Golden Gate Bridge. Now, dry rot has invaded the deck; its aging joists, no longer steady, falter in their tilt toward the earth and its railings have pulled away from the house. The sign on the deck warns *Danger, Do Not Enter.* In like fashion I, too, falter. The spring has gone out of my step, and I weave an unsteady path while my joints mourn the elixir of youth. The face in the mirror appears saggy, a little anguished and devoid of its earlier animation. Sometimes I muster a brilliant smile as if to plead a like response. But the smile cannot hold and the mirror knows there is no going back. So I fix my hair, touch up my face, and set about making arrangements to shore up the house before the rainy season intrudes.

By now, daylight is seeping into the bedroom. I get up and follow my usual routine—a routine that protects me from an aimlessness that shields me from a sadness I'd rather not face. Opposite the window, a curved wall illuminated with tiny lights enfolds photos of Art, of the children, the cover of a *New Yorker* magazine, a few poems, and a photograph of the 14th century inn in Somersetshire where we spent our honeymoon. Tucked in a corner alongside my green pill container is Art's watch, which is still running.

Upstairs, the house and I greet each other in silent approbation. There are no walls in the dining/kitchen area, which is open to the living room above. Standing for a moment in the quiet space, a certain calm flows into my body and settles into my bones. I sense the ingathering of inerasable love between the living and the departed. This is my quotidian link with Art and with others who passed through this house. It is my no-fear zone where I am protected within an impermeable membrane, a place where danger cannot penetrate.

This protection was with me the day jackhammers were drilling into the street outside the house as city trucks clattered to and fro with workers working, or watching others work. It was sewer repair time. I was busy preparing an early dinner for friends prior to a poetry reading at Cody's Books on Telegraph Avenue. Around four p.m. the trucks and most of the workers had left and I rested on my bed listening to Bach. Afterward, I rejuvenated my face and sped upstairs to fix guacamole and collect the mail. I was halfway back up the front stairs when it hit me that the carport was empty of my blue Honda. At such moments the brain doubts the eyes, so I retraced my steps and checked once again. The carport was indeed empty, except for a few oil stains darkening the concrete.

The Berkeley policeman followed me through the house and down into my bedroom, then casually asked where I keep the keys to my car. With unerring confidence, I told him that they were in my handbag on my desk. Minutes later, the contents of my bag now scattered around the desk, I admitted that my keys were not where I had put them. Unnerved I searched for my wallet but that too had disappeared. My imagination took over. My identity formerly represented by all those numbers stamped on cards and neatly tucked into my wallet had gone missing. I was a non-person. Downstairs in the basement we found the cobwebbed-covered door to the outside wide open.

The burglar had entered through the basement, opened the door to the bedroom, found my keys and wallet, and had driven off with my car. It was clear that he had been hiding in the large walk-in closet in my bedroom while I was relaxing on the bed. Later, I found his muddy footprints on the closet floor together with bottles of pills from a nearby drawer.

The police found my car early the following morning in downtown Oakland. The radio hammering rock music, its two occupants blissfully drunk, the car a mess of bottles and trash. As I hung up the telephone after thanking the police, my relief was linked with a sense of disappointment, since I had secretly admired the calculated audacity of that thief. Now, I was going back to life in my house across from the park, and, he, in an act of self-destruction, was going back to the cold confines of prison. In a confused way, I felt sad for him.

* * *

The fog has lifted since my morning call from Jen, and I'm in the garden, soothed by the sensual warmth of the sun. Ten years ago, in my early eighties, I'd jump out of bed, self-soothed, and ready to plunge ahead. Now, my awakening mind is sometimes tuned to a disquietude that hovers over me in an amorphous cloud. If I bypass my mind and move within, I touch an emotion that is akin to fear, which I quickly dismiss as a general malaise of the very elderly. But I know that's not true. The emotion that beclouds my days has been around many times before, in variant disguises, waiting to be translated into the language of awareness.

The telephone rings and this time it's Jon, calling from his morning hike in the hills above Los Angeles. During the uncertain years between his second and third marriages, we'd follow an undeviating script: Jon: "You O.K. Mum?" Me: "I'm fine, and you?" Jon: "Just fine." But mostly he was not fine. He was lonely for the woman he insisted did not exist. A woman who knew herself, a woman who saw through his quirky moods and still loved him. And so we'd talk consoling talk. He'd console me for the aches and pains of old age, and I'd endeavor to give him hope, adding that I couldn't die before he found his perfect mate, so please make haste. He'd counter with the resolve to put the whole search off, since he wasn't ready for orphan hood. Things change, however, and late one evening as we were talking, he remarked, somewhat jocularly, that it was fine for me to depart now, then suggested that I say hello to "a person who'd just walked in." Thus it was that I met Ann, my third daughter-in-law. They were married here in the garden one sunny June day: Ann, elegant in a blue silk sheath, high heels and sparkles in her hair; and Jon—well, Jon was Jon, dressed in blue jeans, a cotton shirt and, as a concession to Ann, a new pair of tennis shoes. It was a union blessed with the orthodoxy of the true non-believer, and one of the happiest weddings I've witnessed.

* * *

Early afternoon and I've just said good-bye to my cleaning crew. We've been together for over ten years. On alternate Thursdays they clatter up my steps with their heavy equipment, open the front door and call, "Hi, Joan," and the house and I murmur our gratitude. On hot days, the crew sweating and panting from those thirty steps, they drop their bags and vacuum cleaner on the dining room floor. Sometimes they look at me with a kind of wonder—or is it pity?— and ask how I still make it up with my groceries. I assure them that it's good for my legs. I do not tell them that the steps, in a conspiracy with the general landscape are upping the ante, which I fear all too soon, I might not be able to meet.

In a bliss of quietude, I make tea and reflect on the balancing act between the pleasurable sense of community and the profound relief of aloneness. I wonder, as I tilt more toward the solitary, if I'm retreating into a passive self-centeredness. But to do otherwise feels like a willful regression to a distant past, when time was unending and death was a subway station where no one got off.

* * *

These days, I watch as I enter the season of my ditherings. Once a center of firm resolution, I am more forgetful, less focused, and beset with unexplained mood swings. Occasionally people still greet me with, "Oh, you're such a model for your age." And I think I should enlighten them as to its inherent difficulties. Instead I thank them and wonder if they speak with an honest heart or are uttering yet another consolatory, well-worn phrase. Perhaps, though, it is my heart that is less than honest, since I rarely admit to moments when, without warning, my energy drops

10

to the point of non-existence, as if I've sprung a leak and must lie down before I fall down. At ninety-two, energy is the lodestar within which I exist, and when it sinks below my horizon, I too sink into an involuntary quiescence. As I ease into a Zen-like peace, I catch a sense of relief, and the thought that comes is this: perhaps my diminution of energy is part of evolution's innate wisdom, a gradual withdrawal from the pulsing, outer world into the inner realm of pure self. I soon learn, however, that meeting up with the inner self is not necessarily orderly or gentle, but can be abrupt and violent.

* * *

The heavy rain from last night's storm leaked through skylights in my computer room and soaked the pages of writing I'd struggled with all week. Water left its mark on dictionaries, files, unused computer paper, stationery, stamps, and a morass of "stuff" stacked on a converted ping-pong table that serves as an extra desk. My next door neighbor and her husband were to drop in for champagne at five p.m. to celebrate her ninety-third birthday, and I hastened to place containers under the still-leaking roof before puddles on the floor drifted downward into the dining room. Rolling back the carpet behind my computer chair, in order to mop up the water, was the last conscious act I remember.

* * *

When I open my eyes, I am lying on my back on the floor, and for a stunned moment wonder where I am. There is a stillness within the room. Time has arrested its flight. The room takes shape and I try to move, but my right leg just hangs there limply, like a tattered sail attached to a broken mast. Blood trickles down my arms and onto my hands. I feel no pain, nothing. My mind clears and I realize I must have flipped backward over that rolled up rug and, on the way down, met the nearby wooden chaise lounge. Unable to move, I lay there searching the room as if it holds the answer to my dilemma. Then, my mind slips into its organizing mode: How to get from A: the floor, to B: the chair, and finally to C: the telephone. The plan is to wedge my computer chair with its flexible wheels up against my desk, on top of which is a telephone. The chair is out of reach, but by twisting face-down onto the floor and pleading with every strained muscle, I inch closer, until my arm takes off on its own and, with one blessed touch, the chair moves exactly as planned, smack against the desk. Lying immobilized on the floor, I contemplate that waiting chair above me, and recognize a certain kinship—that we are somehow in this together. At the same time, I feel there is no way on this earth I can get up and into it. It is then the voice in my head speaks: *Close your eyes, take a deep breath, and jump.* Opening my eyes, I find myself sitting squarely on the chair, unruffled, as if I'd been reclining there, on any other day, awaiting the arrival of a friend with whom to share a cup of tea. Except on this day, I've gashed open my head and broken my hip.

Later, answering the inevitable question as to what happened, I recount the exact events and my closest friends have no problem understanding. Others, I feel, politely withhold their views as to my sanity, and are merely relieved at my recovery. It is suggested that the jump from floor to chair was adrenalin inspired, alerted by a vigilant unconscious. A physician I queried did not entirely disagree, but he also believes there exists an elemental force, an enfolding presence, that protects us at times of infinite danger. The paranormal is a touchy subject for many, but not for me, since that quiet, unequivocal voice in my head, to which I am sometimes unfaithful, has been with me for most of my adult life. Rooted in my center, it is twin to my deepest self.

* * *

As I write this, three months later, I am drawn back to the precise moment I arrived up there on that chair— to the ordinariness of it all, as if I'd been privy to an agreed blueprint.

I am left with the indelible impression of having experienced a gap in time, during which consciousness was held in abeyance; its shine, momentarily opaque. Meantime, my hip is happy with its titanium implant and my psyche, which faltered with the specter of the dreaded dependency, is back on its unpredictable track.

There is, though, a subtle shift in the play of my days. The fall shook loose a self-image that I've long pursued of a woman endowed with a lively mind, who dances her walk with unflinching invincibility. Part of me still holds this image, but it's countered now by the veritable presence of myself, as I tread more gently and move with less swagger. And, like many older women, at times I must cling to a cane. I'm aware, too, of a new vulnerability in my interaction with others; of my fear that I am viewed with a touch of pity for my increasing fragility; of their disappointment that the expected glow has dimmed to its vanishing point. As I seesaw between these two images, unwilling to relinquish the old and unhappy to accept the new, I realize that the choice is not mine. But that both are here to stay, both will continue to change, since change—that feared intruder who creeps into my well-guarded house—is embedded in our every heartbeat.

* * *

For some, change is embraced as a baptism of renewal, a chance to escape from the existential exactitude of everyday life. But for me, the faintest nudge out of my familiar path and my foundations begin their inexorable disappearing act into a quicksand of fear. There is, always the enemy "out there," as it was three weeks ago on Good Friday. Upon waking, I followed my usual routine, listened to the news, dressed and exercised. Glancing in the mirror, I noticed my early-morning not-yet-together face appeared stranger than usual, and realized that my left eye had disappeared behind a blurry facade. Upstairs, reading the *New York Times* at breakfast, I sat blinking under a bright light, trying to fill in the tops of words to the left of each column, since they, too, had been

13

decapitated. My fear softened somewhat as the accommodating mind slowly filled in each empty space and I felt a guarded hope of optimism that this sudden change was a temporary aberration. Later, the MRI showed that I'd had a small stroke—a little bit of me had floated up and landed into the visual area of my brain.

Late afternoon, I sit at the dining room table and gaze onto the garden. Bay Area fog disappeared early today, usurped by a singularly ardent sun, and the house, the garden and I sink into a collective stupor. There is a certain tranquility in a heat-induced exhaustion, and with my batteries down to a shade above zero, there is no energy to be anywhere other than in this exact moment. No energy to listen to the trickster-mind with its contrived fears, its concoctions sent to tantalize, to confound, and perhaps to grow me. I keep company only with the empty moment. I hear the crows calling as they swoop across the trees, hear the children in the park, smell the smoke of barbecues. In the stillness I feel the garden merge into me, so that the garden is pulsating within me. The garden, the house, and I hum to the same melody. I am reminded that when I do not look, is when I see. And when I do not listen, is when I hear. And when I do not think, I am.

A Different Woman

Untwisting all the chains that tie
The hidden soul of harmony.

John Milton

"Would you want Leo back?" I asked Marta. Widows for almost five years, Marta and I sat drinking tea in my dining room. Along the wall behind the tables, photos of Art reside in proprietary grace, his lively, amused gaze following me around the house we built. After posing the question to Marta, though, I felt I'd uttered an unforgivable blasphemy. I wanted to bow apologetically in front of each of Art's photos, to stroke his face in my hands, in the hope that repentance would bring forgiveness and obliterate the heresy of my thoughts. Deep down I knew it was myself I was questioning.

Marta's reply was ambivalent. Her marriage to Leo had known profound love and loyalty and fierce disagreement. Their in-house battles had centered around the issues of control; in Argentina, the country of their birth, the males of their generation assumed a dominance that had not sat gently with Marta. Since Leo's death, however, with no vetoes to trouble a long-held dream, Marta transformed the gloomy living space of her house into an all-windowed sun-catching studio, and replaced the concrete-covered backyard with an exotic flower garden. The antiquated kitchen, liberated from its shadowed corner, now occupied the center of the house, flaunting a sleek unaccustomed modernity.

Marta's voice held no equivocation as she confessed that for the first time in thirty-five years she felt a sense of unparalleled freedom. I sat back—the attentive listener—awed by her honesty, happy this was her expose and not mine. Then I poured myself another cup of tea and basked in the complacency of my own more perfect marriage.

For weeks afterward, the word *freedom* kept flashing on and off in my brain like the security light that scans the outside of my house at night, and I could no longer hide what I had long known. I have become a different woman since Art has died. Though Art had brought untold bliss to my life—without him I have known raw, immobilizing grief—the freedom I'm living now is one I'd find hard to surrender. It's as if the cocoon of marital comfort in which I was happily indulged for so many years burst asunder, catapulting me into a new world where I might fly to a distant star or sink to a waiting grave. Flying, however, is not without its terrors.

* * *

Uneasiness began to haunt my days and wreck my nights, and then guilt moved in as I wondered if it were possible for love and freedom to coexist within a marriage. Perhaps this is simply a philosophical abstraction, but it has become less so since Art has died. Unable to face my conflicted feelings, I deviously continued to question my women friends about the freedom in their marriages. In her sixties, Rita, whose second marriage was proving as troublesome as her first, had no hesitation in describing the institution of marriage as a prison. Elizabeth and Ann, in their eighties, were somewhat ruffled by my question and murmured only that they remembered Art as the kindest and least demanding of men. The screw turned another notch deeper into my psyche.

Memories from the past have their way of drifting into a present perplexity, and I am back twenty years to the time of Art's retirement, to a time when I was changing from an aiming-to-please extrovert, to a woman whose greatest solace was to rest more in her own aloneness. Together sharing a quiet breakfast, spending much of the day apart, and together again for dinner was my ideal plan. While Art, with his unfailing empathy and love, accepted my needs as best he could, I felt profoundly selfish and lived with an abiding guilt.

Chastened and distraught by unresolved doubt, I scheduled an appointment with Amos, the Buddhist therapist I occasionally visit whose quiet observations invariably move me out of confusion and back into understanding. The following Wednesday afternoon I sat opposite him and wept. Did my present feelings of freedom imply a past entrapment? Had my fifty-two years of serenity with Art been merely a fantasy of a needy imagination? And what about my scarring guilt?

"You're talking about two entirely separate issues," Amos asserted, "your guilt, and your marriage." Slowly I began to understand that my guilt had nothing at all to do with Art and the quality of our marriage. Rather it was the guilt of self-deception, of denying what is mine. The reason I feel free is simply because I am. It is a freedom conceived in love and made viable through loss.

My life with Art was one in which we fostered each other's needs, smoothed one another's rough spots and lived our subscribed roles. Helpless when faced with a broken appliance, a stuck typewriter ribbon, a recalcitrant car that refused to start, I'd simply call Art who would unerringly fix the problem. Likewise, in social situations where I knew Art might wish he were elsewhere, I'd see his face as he searched the room for me and I'd immediately rescue him. Neither of us intruded across party lines and it worked for us. But, at the same time, we protected each other from pushing against our growing edges and part of me willingly relaxed into an extended gestation that could only be born after Art died.

The other day, nervously cutting down invasive bamboo trees in the garden, I felt Art there, keeping a watchful eye on me. The stems varied in length from twenty to thirty feet and as they fell, I prayed they would not decapitate a rose bush. Then I heard Art's encouraging voice: *See, I told you you could do it.* And I stood there wondering about my assumed helplessness when we were together.

As a child I had not dared to look at the danger that lurked in the emotional darkness of my home. My father was having affairs; my mother's desperation loomed like a simmering volcano, and my family was unraveling around me. I learned never to ask questions of my parents, since if I did, they might confirm my worst fears and abandon me, leaving no forwarding address. And then who would be there for me? Better not to know anything, I reasoned.

It was only during my marriage to Art that I began to wonder about the nature of the world around me—how it had started, how the planets were formed—questions an inquisitive child would ask. Endowed with godlike patience, Art would explain his theories to me and for one shining moment I'd hear, and understand, before my mind would drift back into its studied lethargy—into that tug-of-war between my desire to know and my intractable gut fighting to remain ignorant.

Ironically, though, the battleground changed after Art died. Blind grief shocked me out of my habitual rut and my mind jump-started to a different rhythm. As I took hold of life again in a less shuttered state, I began to explore the unknown with a more receptive, less quivering heart. There was nothing to fear now, since the worst had happened and I was still alive.

Two weeks after Art died, his colleague Seth telephoned to offer me comfort. Hearing Seth's voice, my mood jumped into high alert, the way it used to whenever we chanced to meet at concerts or parties. About twenty years ago at a dinner party with Art, I watched Seth arrive—a seasoned performer—dressed in a black turtleneck with a sweater casually draped over his shoulders. Alongside him stood his wife, a beauty beyond measure, with whom he was rarely seen. It appeared that they lived their lives separately, unconstrained by convention. On this particular occasion she was majestic in her boredom and I sensed that she was there under pressure. Later, as people mingled after dinner, I found her sitting next to me and though we'd never met before, she raged like a furious Medea against academia, the institution of marriage, and in particular against Seth. This was not a two-way conversation and I didn't interrupt, but I was aware of an overwhelming urge to defend this man who was being defamed. At the same time I suspected that her anger toward him was not entirely misplaced. In hindsight, I realized that what held me in thrall was Seth's resemblance to my father. My love affairs during my teens and early twenties invariably involved charismatic older men. Given the slimmest resemblance, I'd fit them into a projection of my idealized father—the father who would cherish me, who would never leave me.

During the phone call, Seth who was now widowed invited me out for coffee. I suggested to him that we have tea at my house instead. On the deck above the garden, we sat talking about Art. As I studied Seth's face I felt the old attraction—coupled with an uneasy excitement—stir within me. The conversation turned to his concern about how I would manage living alone. Would I remain in the house? Were my children around and supportive? As we talked my grief moved silently into the shadows, and I came face-to-face with the teenager who coveted the forbidden, the almost adult who had not yet learned the art of discernment.

During the next six months, Seth came to tea a few more times and each time I lost more of my uneasiness. In September, I invited him to dinner. As I stood in the kitchen awaiting his arrival, I was assailed by a grief as intense as any I could remember. I needed Art right there with me, to touch me, to tell me who I was. Then Art's voice, which is everywhere, told me to walk forward, to not look back. I heard Seth coming up the steps. In a kind of frozen obedience, I opened the door and smiled my welcome. I was back in the now. We sat outside for a while in the warmth of the evening, sipping our wine and chatting with the studied intimacy of contenders in a friendly game of chess. Meantime, my unsettled self was hinting that it might be a fine idea for a small earthquake to abruptly end the evening. Later, at the dinner table, soothed by the soporific effects of wine and food and, no less, by the man sitting next to me, I had the uncanny sensation of expanding into a lighter space. In some magical manner, I had tossed overboard a layer of baggage that had outlived its time. After dinner, as we listened to music upstairs in the living room, Seth talked about his conflicted marriage, his views on the imperfections of monogamy, and his delight in the company of women. In turn, I emphasized the blessedness of my many years with Art, adding that I had no wish to marry again—though perhaps I might take a lover. It was a calculated remark, and Seth's quick rejoinder was to the point. "Let's take off our clothes," he ventured.

Caught in a web of my own design, my mind was sounding its familiar warnings, and I panicked. I hoped to find an easy exit. I looked into Seth's face, but saw only impassivity and his lingering question. Playing for time, I got up from the couch, walked across the room, and switched off the music. Then my attendant heart moved to my rescue. "Let's," I replied, turning back to Seth.

Downstairs in the bedroom it was more than my clothes I took off. I also let go of a script written by a triad of enforcers: twentieth century middle-class England, where sex was a blushingly dirty word; my parents, whose sexual war games bruised my innocence; and finally, perhaps most importantly, my conforming self who had learned to bury her sexuality under a colossus of shame. Art and I had loved each other for fifty-two years and our lovemaking had been a shared delight, yet we both had known part of me remained in hiding. I had taken my mother's mantra too much to heart. "To trust your love to a man is the surest path to abandonment," she would say. After I lost Art, the terrible grief that burst through all of my withholdings liberated parts of myself I'd never known. At the age of eighty, I was to meet them.

My relationship with Seth is, I tell him, my great experiment. He calls me on every one of my tightly held protections, and his pleasure in meeting my body is matched by my freedom to respond. Ours is a relationship with no hidden agenda and no commitments. Our occasional evenings of uncomplicated delight are the intertwining of two desires who embrace one another, knowing they will meet again sometime, somewhere. And while sex is not absent from our meetings, it is rather my compelling ache to be touched and to be held, and to touch and to hold that pulls me back each time to Seth. Like the newly born whose being depends upon the enfolding presence of a parent, those of us who are now so old, glow more warmly when we, too, may share our tenderness.

Though my life is still very much a solitary one, my imagination gifts the empty spaces with the fantasy that one day, returning home from the market, I will open the front door and find Art waiting for me upstairs in the living room, lounging in his favorite leather chair, wearing the green velour jacket we bought together.

"There she is," he says, as he swivels the chair in my direction, the way he always did.

I leave the groceries in the kitchen, walk the six steps up to the living room and Art stands to greet me. I take his bearded face in my hands and speak his name, our natures merging in this moment of pure enchantment.

Yes, I want him back, every second of every hour. But it would be different.

The Gentle Art of Dying

Do not go gentle into that good night...
Rage, rage against the dying of the light.

Dylan Thomas

Each Friday, Beth arrives for lunch, clinging hand over hand to the railing alongside the forty steps that lead up to my house. Her unrestrained ebullience, along with her vocation as a therapist who once nurtured innumerable souls, has petered out, leaving her rudderless in unfamiliar territory and with a sense of shame that she has, once again, forgotten the answer to the question she just asked. We sit side by side in my living room where I read poems by Rilke or T.S. Eliot, or passages from books we've read together over the years. Occasionally we have warm discussions the way we used to, though most often Beth floats away into the comfort of oblivion. But she never loses her sense of joy. Standing in my garden she marvels as the resident squirrel jumps from the Japanese maple onto the bird feeder in one infallible leap. She points as a humming bird hovers over the scarlet Salvia bush. Things I look at but never see. After we eat lunch, I guide her downstairs to my bedroom where she immediately falls asleep, hugging my pillow like a trusting child. At ninety-five, she is asleep now more often than she is awake. I stand by the side of the bed watching Beth, who is wearing bright blue pants, a yellow sweatshirt and a jazzy pair of mismatched socks, and feel the chilling despair of imminent loss.

At my age, an irrevocable exodus of people I cherish meld into a processional of pilgrims, venturing into the unknown. When queried, I reply that I do not dwell much on my own leaving. But increasingly, as I listen to the unceasing narrative in my mind, I catch an errant thought that wonders when I'll join the procession, and I hear my heart answer, somewhat testily, that I have too many unfinished projects and, surely, there's no hurry. Sometimes I ask myself if I'm pleading for some kind of a postponement that will favor me with the gift of time, since time, that social conceit within which we all live, is the final arbiter of our existence. The older I become, the faster time accelerates until, some day, I know it will disappear and I with it.

The finitude of life is not a topic to enliven most social gatherings, but at lunch this afternoon with three friends it seems quite natural. Sue, Susan, Janet and I met as Hospice volunteers twenty years ago, an intimacy that has never stopped. Sitting around my dining room table, eating spinach and goat cheese pizza, still reflecting on the passage of time, I bring up the question of when the process of dying actually begins. When we're handed a terminal diagnosis? upon reaching our prescribed growth? with our first life affirming birth-cry? The four of us agree that to be brain dead is the legal definition of death, but none of us can come up with a definition as to the onset of dying. We decide to give it some thought before our next meeting and then sustain ourselves with another helping of dessert, before discussing more worldly subjects.

Later as the garden falls, exhausted from the delights of an over-ardent sun, I sit on the porch and watch the fog move in from across the Bay. Listening to the fog horn's ghostly lament, I shiver a little the way I used to sometimes when thinking about Art who died almost eight years ago. I remember those tender last years when he didn't know he was dying, and then how quickly he left. Or did he know he was dying? The Welsh poet Dylan Thomas's blistering poem about his father's death beats its inexorable rhythm in my mind, and I wish I could write the poet a letter, wherever he might be, to tell him that he got it all wrong. To rage against dying only makes the journey unnecessarily perilous. He should know, since he's been there.

The rainy season is my writing season. I sit at the computer in my studio as rain thunders down onto the skylight, such that I cannot easily hear a telephone conversation. The garden is soaked and the surrounding bamboos sway endearingly, like supplicating courtiers, while the neighbor's cat crouches under my back porch. This light-filled room holds my wellspring of contentment, where books are my dearest companions and the red Oriental rug comforts my meditation. Today, though, unlike the elements, I am not flowing. Frozen in front of my computer screen, which confronts me like an insatiable Hydra, I have no offerings, no well-tuned phrases, only a mind wholly fixated on that unanswered question from last month's lunch with my Hospice friends.

Two hours into my abyss of nothingness, I turn off the computer and escape into the kitchen to bake cookies I do not need. I suspect my mind is indulging its familiar pattern of chicanery, a ploy I use when my comfort level is threatened. Two hours and four-dozen cookies later, the storm relents both outside and inside, and I realize that my concern is not at all about the onset of dying, but rather about my personal odyssey with time itself. It is about how I live my dying, whenever its genesis.

Perhaps I am less honest than I'm willing to admit about my leaving. Friends greet me frequently these days with the question: How is your health? No longer the uncomplicated: How are you? And I fear that to the outward eye I'm fast-forwarding. Times when my courage is high, a check with the mirror confirms the unvarnished truth: my body, like the exterior of an ancient edifice, is yielding to the demands of gravity. For nearly nine decades my body and I have been partners in an adventure of mutual caring and consolation. We have repaired our wounds and continued the dance, refining our choreography to temper the moment. But to jump out of bed with the insouciance of a ballerina is no longer in the repertoire. Instead, I orchestrate each successive move to cajole hesitant bones toward the vertical position. I concentrate on the ins and outs of my breath, and relax every muscle. I edge toward the side of the bed, a stratagem that foils the assault of debilitating leg cramps. The pattern in place, I resolutely swing to standing. And so it goes throughout the day, each movement a rehearsed pas de deux performed by inseparable friends, my breath and me.

These days, alert to my body's changing path, I am compelled to be extra vigilant. My nose tends to drip without my awareness, and well-trained muscles are a little weary, so that a burst of laughter can produce an embarrassing leak, never mind the gas I manufacture which has a mind of its own. At such times, I pray my friends are as deaf as I am. Left with a growing frustration at my body's increasing inadequacies, I wonder how much longer it will accommodate its load. "What ifs?" invade my nights. Morbid fantasies shred my faith in the body as a miracle of self-repair. Seth, who was once a champion squash and tennis player, and is now barely able to walk, came to dinner last week. Later, gathering up his coat and walking stick, he hugged me goodbye and told me, rather belligerently, to close the door and to not watch his confrontation with the steps.

The piece of work entitled 'Me' (or Thou) carries no fixed date of completion. For much of my life, I performed on stage like a moth fluttering toward the light. In older age, though, no longer desperate for approbation, in part due to waning energy, but more (I like to think) to having let go of past attachments, my role has mutated from that of the observed to that of the observer, a benign witness who rests on the sidelines, watching the uncensored version of me being me.

I watch myself behave like an octogenarian. About to climb the steep steps to my dentist's office, I hesitate as I notice an acquaintance I've known for thirty years contemplating the challenge of descent. She holds onto a metal, triangular walking stick which she waves at me to say, come on up. We meet at the top and she greets me with, "I'm ninety-five, you know, and stairs can be quite a problem." To which I reply, somewhat apologetically, "I'm only 87 but indeed they can." We commiserate further about our wayward balance, congratulate ourselves on still being ambulatory, and complain at the intrusion of medical appointments into our social life. We end our conversation in amicable agreement that our minds are still intact. Though we have, of course, forgotten each other's names.

Perhaps this unremitting focus on age carries within it a plea of forgiveness for our sins of omission—like deafness, impaired eyesight, and a slackened memory. Increasingly I announce my age with almost Biblical pride and wait for the expected reassurance from a friend, No, you can't be! That's impossible. Should I hear only a polite acceptance, I wither. But my point is not so much the unavoidable slippage of our senses, rather it's the subject matter of our conversations. We have become totally body oriented: aching knees, arthritic fingers, stiffened hips, gastric reflux.... Items on an agreed agenda, we listen to each other with empathy (sometimes with disguised pleasure) before turning to more lively topics. I suspect this emphasis on growing infirmities derives from an unconscious fear that moves us to tender our body, and to hug it as we would a tired child.

Yet fear also seeks the light and, given an invitation, it will dart into awareness, agitating the still waters of our landscape. Writing about living and dying, I am an unwitting host to a family of diverse emotions who sit with me in my writing room, like inscrutable, smiling Buddhas, as I struggle to articulate their message.

Writing is a solitary occupation and, lacking the protective warmth of friends, I'm easily thrown into abject forlornness and the conviction that I'm an inconsequential speck on a frozen planet. Today, though, I'm not forlorn, only increasingly frustrated at my prevaricating, since I have spent the entire weekend trying to avoid hearing what my uninvited guests wish to tell me. I don't want to think about a time when I will not be around; when another family will live in this house of a thousand delights; when my garden will be loved by strangers; when people will ask…Is she still alive? The way I ask about distant friends. I don't want to think about my non-being. But I do.

I also think about my last moments with my children and grandchildren and my cherished friends, and how to speak to them from my heart. Little etherized poetics come to mind. But these are only for me, to blur the unbearable grief of separation. And I wonder how best to tell them that without this grieving, I would have lived a desiccated life devoid of love, since grief is inseparable from love. That life and death are woven out of a common fabric: that the design of our living is the design of our dying.

A Farewell

Between the pairs of opposites must the world
suffer without ceasing. The opposites together form God.

The Upanishads

I stayed close behind Art as we walked down our front steps to the car that Wednesday morning. He looked huddled, scared and terribly alone. The pain around his heart had left him bewildered and struggling for breath. As we drove to the Emergency Room at Alta Bates Hospital, I wanted to console him, hug him, search his face for hope. But I didn't. We had momentarily cut off from one another as if to shield ourselves from the intrusion of unthinkable thoughts. Lovers for fifty-two years, neither of us dared contemplate the language of separation. At a deep level I sensed this was the prelude to a farewell.

* * *

There were omens. Three weeks earlier we were reading the newspaper over breakfast when Art stood up, walked into the dining room and then wandered back into the kitchen. He repeated this route a few more times and then, looking puzzled, sat down at the end of the table away from his usual place across from me. I asked him if he was all right and after a long pause he said that he couldn't understand a word he was reading. He spoke slowly and with difficulty as if a connection was missing between his thoughts and his speech. It was the first time I ever saw fear in his eyes. Sitting there at the table, looking at each other, I felt the apprehensions of a gathering storm, but said nothing; for to name the feeling would give it form and I wasn't ready. Tests would show that Art had had a slight stroke and would recover quickly. Days passed, and he seemed to lose his fear. But I didn't lose mine. I never stopped watching him.

* * *

Driving the familiar streets of Berkeley toward Alta Bates Hospital, I felt Art and I were playing roles in a drama about another elderly couple, certainly not us. On Shattuck Avenue we stopped for a red light, and for a few seconds reality intervened and my fear broke through. I almost turned the car around, as if by retracing our route back home I could somehow obliterate the truth. I wanted to hold Art in my arms and ask him not to leave— not just now. As the light changed, Art started to hum a tune, a habit of his when stressed. He continued humming in the crowded Emergency Room to the delight of another patient, a young woman who smiled at each new song.

Emergency Rooms are unquiet places, full of emotions, suppressed or otherwise, and I averted my eyes from the other patients, not wishing to empathize with their distress. I was having my own troubles, stifling an immanent earthquake roiling around inside my gut. The blood tests came back and showed that Art's heart attack was not too serious and would respond to medication. It was decided that he would stay overnight in order for his heart to be monitored, and I would pick him up early the next day. Our fears stilled, we hugged each other in our usual way and I left for home.

The next morning John, our family doctor for over twenty-five years, called to tell me that he'd just visited Art who was confused and had not recognized him. It appeared that Art had suffered a cerebral hemorrhage that left him brain damaged, unable

30

to speak and blind in one eye. A neurologist had been called in for consultation and John suggested that I return to the hospital as soon as possible. I dressed in my brightest clothes, made my face up, ate breakfast and phoned the children. I had momentarily clocked out. Whenever my heart is threatened, I move with robotic obedience out of the compartment marked feeling and into the one marked thinking. It's a move that happens as surely as my next breath, a habit that's been with me all my life. Driving alone to the hospital, I thought about the hug Art and I had shared the night before, and wondered how he would look today with one unseeing eye, speechless and unable to laugh his laugh. Would he know me? In my mind, I practiced my entry into his room.

The neurologist was with Art when I got there. I immediately took Art's hands into mine and looked into his face. He struggled to speak and the sounds he made were unintelligible. His face held the baffled look of an uncomprehending child. I looked deeply into his good eye, and sensed he knew me, though we were unable to connect through a wall that was slowly separating his world from mine. My heart constricted into a tighter knot as I watched Art in that hospital bed slip further into a coma, seemingly unaware of my presence. I thought about the quality of life that would be left for him in any future. For the past eight years he had lived valiantly with prostate cancer, which had metastasized into his bones. What if he were dragged back into life—a voiceless captive to his pain? Art loved life, loved the simple pleasures of watching the garden, the birds fluttering around our feeder, the deer hungry for our roses. He could spend hours in sitting solitude. But this world would be like a dark existence that I knew would have its agonies. How could I know Art's limits? Or was I thinking of my own? Would I remain loving, compassionate and tender? Or would I escape into anger and resentment?

Perhaps it didn't matter, since I was mindful of Art's decision a few years earlier when we wrote our Living Wills. They explicitly stated that in the event of disabling illness, which would make the quality of life unbearable, he wished not to be resuscitated. Art's breathing was louder now, more agitated, and I didn't stop to ponder the meaning of 'unbearable.' I asked our doctor to let him go gently. And my heart began its long winter of hibernation.

We were moved into a room on the sixth floor away from the hubbub of the nursing floor. A cavernous room once used for storage, it now held two twin beds, a table and one worn arm-chair. The night nurse was to check in on us every hour, but otherwise Art and I would be left alone. Standing at the end of Art's bed, I studied his face as if it was that of a stranger. I touched his pulse and felt the steady drumming of his heart beating its loud farewells, his every breath a crescendo of embat-tled sound taking over the room. There was Art and there was me and there was this sound. And what if it should stop?

All that night I stayed with him. I held his hand, which was no longer responsive to mine, hands that would never stroke me again. From time to time I spoke his name, hoping that he would sense my presence as he was leaving. Around midnight I moved onto his bed. I rested my face against his and thought of things I wished I'd told him yesterday in the Emergency Room: how his love for me had spun an incandescence around my heart which would never dim. How the joy of our life together on this earth would comfort the despair of his leaving. I wished that I had told him that this separation is but a pause in our continuum.

I needed to say goodbye, yet I couldn't find the words. A large clock hung high on the wall above Art's bed was the only thing with a purpose. The second hand made its steady course, knowing exactly where it was going. But did I? Toward morning Art's breathing became quieter and then, like an evanescent breeze passing through, it ceased. And he left.

I held him as his body changed from warm to cool to cold, then I moved onto the chair where I stayed for another two hours, guarding him, phantom-like, in that silent room. I had no thoughts, no emotions. I was simply a lingering proto-plasm attached to an old chair. Perhaps I was waiting for Art to wake up. As the room grew lighter, I heard the arrival of the morning shift and my mind told me it was time to leave. At the door I turned for one last look, imprinting Art's face into my soul. And then I left.

* * *

Over the years I had spent many hours at Alta Bates Hospital; this is where I did my hospice work, where I had once been part of a warm community. The morning Art died, however, I made my way zombie-like through the building as the hospital staff began its early-morning activities. I felt I was part of the walking dead. My feelings muted within the solace of shock, I carried a yellow plastic hospital bag containing Art's clothes and shoes, his hairbrush and watch. I think my daughter Jennifer drove me home, but all I remember now is that yellow plastic bag and my feelings of guilt over leaving Art upstairs in that storage room with nobody to hold his coldness. When I got home, I walked downstairs into our bedroom and pushed the yellow bag deep into a drawer in Art's dresser. It would be three months before I could open that drawer.

My blurred image of the rest of the day is one of friends bringing food and flowers, and of endless telephone calls. With a slightly manic edge, our house seemed to be in perpetual motion. People hugged and consoled me as I attempted to respond. But the self who had held Art's hand while he sang his songs just three days earlier was gone. I had become an automaton performing the requisite rituals associated with the ending of a life. Four miles away, Art was a body lying in a mortuary, waiting to be fired into ash.

That night I stood at the foot of our king-sized bed, hesitant to enter, and looked at its familiar indentations of shared occupancy. Art had built the pine shelves around our bed that held the radio and CD player. CD's he'd been listening to were still in the player, books lying open at his place of reading. Art had the habit of reading several books at a time, many stacked on top of one another, on the shelf above our bed, some ending up on the floor. I smelled the lingering scent of intimacy redolent of sweet musk, which clung to Art's pillow, and saw grief waiting there. But all I knew was an inanimate nothingness. I was not yet ready to grieve. Standing at the foot of our bed, I felt I was teetering at the edge of a thirty-foot diving board with no chance to retreat. Then, assuming a bravery I didn't own, I closed my eyes and jumped.

Hours later, I awoke in a place of otherworldly bliss, embraced in an ocean of beatitude, waves of euphoria flowing through me in orgasmic rhythm, as if to announce the consummation of a love affair with its promise of perpetual sustenance. I felt part of a symphony of perfection where there is no darkness, only a shining luminosity. I have read that man is able to experience pure bliss for only a moment because too much would destroy him. Had it been offered to me that night, I would have taken the chance. The next morning the bliss was still around me, only less intense. And, after a while, it disappeared—leaving behind a blueprint stored in my memory, a remnant of which returns from time to time, touching me gently and lightening my sorrow.

I've never understood the kinship between grief and sorrow, but now it is becoming clearer. I'm finding grief to be like a cataclysmic earthquake; it obliterates the landscape, reducing the familiar to desolate rubble and numbing the senses. Whereas sorrow is more like a river, an endless flowing river, at times destructive, flooding its banks, but eventually comforting as it animates its surroundings.

There are still days when no matter what I do or where I wander, there is no river and only detritus from the earthquake, and I am lost for a time in a dry, familiar stuck place. I am learning, however, to wait awhile until the river flows again and my heart, carrying my tears, finds its slow way home.

Paris

There are more things in heaven and earth, Horatio
Than are dreamt of in your philosophy.

William Shakespeare

In your eighties falling in love is easy. Go to Paris. Go with a daughter who wants to celebrate her 50th birthday with you. Go with a questing heart.

Set in my ways, at first I turned down Jennifer's invitation, pleading exigencies of an aging body, uncertain finances and antipathy toward change. Poised and confident in my own surroundings, I fall apart and become mush when in unfamiliar territory. And, besides, this time I would be without Art.

Shortly after Jen's proposal, though, I was invited to dinner at my friends Rita and Bill's house. When I mentioned my daughter's invitation and my reluctance to accept, another guest remarked—quite sharply, I thought—that a mother fortunate enough to be invited by her daughter on such a trip does not turn down the honor. Later, driving home and feeling somewhat cowed, I engaged in a familiar internal debate between the woman who dares and the widow who withers. By the time I pulled my car into the garage, I had changed my mind.

* * *

Jen and I flew to Paris in August, the month most Parisians escape the city's heat, and people like us invade along with every student from everywhere. Arriving at Aéroport Charles de Gaulle eleven hours after leaving San Francisco International on a plane designed for people with uncomplaining legs and slender frames, we wandered outside the terminal in search of a taxi. In my best French, I asked a passing auburn-haired young Colette how to get into Paris, but our conversation was mired in a mutuality of non-comprehension, no doubt partly due to my English accent. A mini-bus driver, overhearing our predicament, offered to drive us to our hotel, though we were not on his designated route.

"Perhaps I can help you," he ventured in English with that French accent that turns me into a pulsating eighteen year old, with visions of Charles Boyer and sublime romance. As he slipped the handle of my suitcase from my hand, I blushed at the audacity of my mind's flirtatious thoughts.

Our apartment was on the third floor of a residential hotel, on rue des Bernardins in the Latin Quarter. The bedroom and living room opened onto balconies lined with pink and red geraniums, and across the street a garden was available to the public until dark, when an elderly gardener arrived to lock the wrought iron gate for the night. It was on this balcony at one a.m. the next morning, that I stood listening to Paris quiet down, wondering what was going on behind all those shuttered apartments across the way on rue Monge. The incessant daytime flux and flow slowed into a hum as the city translated itself into the companionable heartbeat of a satiated lover. Rain glistened the streets as the heat and humidity moved into a cool, forgiving breeze. Standing there, I watched a man leap the garden fence and relieve himself in the bushes and wondered who might, in turn, be watching me, white haired and ghost-like in my flowing pajamas.

The next day I found Paris inhabited by the angelics, friendly vigilantes who kept watch over us as we discovered the jewels they had left behind. After a breakfast of croissants, confiture and fresh apricots, Jen and I queued with the host of tourists in front of Notre Dame, to wait our turn to enter the Cathedral. We were a festive crowd, wilting under a hot sun, besieged by vendors waving postcards in our faces, offering ice cream and maps and copper trinkets. Inside Notre Dame, in the dim light assailed by the fortissimo murmurings of the crowd, I felt strangely isolated, though somehow inspirited by the obscurity. Then my eyes cleared, and they were all there like observing angels—the stonemasons, carpenters, artisans—all toiling day after day, year after year, creating this expression of their faith. Time had magically telescoped the twelfth century into the twentieth, entwining my life with theirs so that we might hear each other's stories.

I stood lost in reverie, remembering when Art and I had visited the Cathedral in 1959, and how I'd obsessed about the people who had built it, wondering about their lives, their loves, their losses. Moving around the nave with Jen, I sensed they were all back with me, and that we understood each other in the manner of old friends who share in a compatibility of silence. Lingering incense heavied the air and the dim flickering points of candlelight— together with the chanting of the faithful at Mass—lent a mysterious, surreal quality to this sacred place. Thoughts of Art floated up again, this time ruffling my quiet, and I was shaken with the interminable grieving of dispossession. Before leaving, I walked to the transept and stood looking at the North and South Rose Windows, feeling a beauty beyond my understanding. As sunlight flooded through the stained glass, illuminating this crown jewel of France, I found a pew reserved for those who wished to pray and sat there and wept.

* * *

Sacré Coeur is a jewel in a different setting. Pristine white, perched high upon a hill in Montmartre, it contemplates Paris as a lover regards a beloved. Walking down its many steps into crowds milling about in the sunshine, I found the Paris of today: accordion

37

players, drummers, guitar-strumming singers, all jamming together in a melange of jazz, rock and African. Next to a stone wall by
the gardens, a cellist played my favorite Bach sonata. Oblivious to
those of us listening, he played with his eyes closed, enchanted as
were we with his heavenly tones. I bent to drop a few francs into
his purse and he opened his eyes and he looked back with a
gorgeous smile, which found my heart and has never left.

Around the side of the Cathedral, a crowd stood watching
a Saint who was at least nine feet tall and enveloped in antique
robes, his face stark white as he stood there deep in prayer. For
over fifteen minutes he moved not a muscle and seemed not even
to breathe. I thought he would surely melt in that incandescent
sun. Then a small child put some money into the collection plate
on the ground and the Saint carefully opened one eye, delivered a
conspiratorial wink, and returned just as suddenly to prayer.

* * *

I have long had a one-sided love affair with M. Claude
Monet. Prints of his water lily series hang on the wall above my
desk at home. Fading through the years, they are promptly replaced
by freshly minted, identical prints. An hour's journey from Paris,
Jennifer and I arrived in the village of Giverny along with the usual
busloads of tourists. Queuing in the humidity of the narrow lane
alongside Monet's studio—now a gift shop—I wondered how
Monet would have viewed our intrusion into his beloved house and
gardens. Were I granted one wish, I would ask for one hour to be
entirely alone in his enchanted garden, to walk along the path to
the water-lily pond and linger on the Japanese bridge, to watch him
in his boat, painting his sublime visions into perpetuity.

* * *

For someone who has little spatial sense, who can only
read a map when it's turned upside-down, the Metro proved quite

a challenge. To manage, I had to know the name of the end-of-the-line stop in the direction in which I was travelling. At night in bed, I would study the map, drawing my own version carefully in black pen. The next morning, I'd wander around the Metro, clutching my homemade directions in my nervous hands. Jennifer, however, preferred to travel map-less. She let her intuitive sense of direction guide us, and would with a few exceptions always get us to the right place. It was the day we had planned to travel across town to visit the Picasso Museum that we had one of our rare mother-daughter problems. Climbing repetitively up and down the unrelenting stairs, unable to find our connection, and feeling limp from the unaccustomed humidity and jostling crowds, I finally yelled, "Why on earth don't you use a map?"

"Why on earth don't you relax a little?" Jen yelled back. That afternoon she saw a new me she'd rather not face: an insecure, old woman whose fear of being lost was tantamount to an early demise; a mother who doubted her daughter. It was not Jen's anger, however, that pierced me, but her accompanying look of naked fury. A few hours later, alone in our apartment before dinner, I thought about the inherent intricacies of the mother/daughter relationship, with its palette of fluctuating hues from warm, soft and glowing, to fierce, binding and destructive. That evening, drinking wine in our kitchen, we talked about our anger, neither of us ceding our initial positions. Though by then our volatility had surrendered to the comfort of our habitual tenderness.

* * *

A touch of class permeates my vision of Paris, albeit a vision seen through a lens of romantic expectations. To walk alongside the Seine at any time of the day does nothing to tarnish my view. Friends greet each other with gentle brushings on both cheeks and lovers kiss with passion, which does not exclude the observer. In California, I avert my eyes from entwined lovers, aware of my embarrassment and their possible ill will. But Paris owns an innocent sensuality that invites participation, enticing me to abandon my more restrained mores. At least while I'm a guest.

Shopping for food in Paris transforms the mundane into the spiritual. No pre-touching the produce of one's choice, no plastic wrapped cheeses, no standing in lines of frenzied shoppers and no automatic have a nice day responses. At Harmon Saisons, the produce market on Place Maubert, I politely pointed to the peaches I desired, not daring to grab the ones I thought most beautiful. In my best French, I listed my wants and they were carefully handed over. The pursuit of food became a solemn undertaking, respect expected on both sides of the counter. At the charcuterie next door, cheese was presented to me on a tiny porcelain dish for tasting, along with scholarly comments which I tried hard to understand. My eggs were placed in my hands with religious gravity, the shopkeeper and I exchanging greetings upon entering and upon leaving, sharing an intimacy of politeness which, in some way, inspirited the groceries I carried back home in my string bag.

A week into our visit, a friend of Jen's arrived from New York to stay at a nearby hotel. Trudging along with my daughter and her friend, Cathy, who with infinite patience adjusted their pace to mine, I began to feel increasingly weary and beset by an intangible sadness.

On Sunday morning, I awakened from a dream that left me feeling abandoned, empty and lost. So I dressed and slipped out quietly to take a solitary walk along the rue des Écoles and toward the produce market on Place Maubert. As I waited to be served, I met Liliane. In her mid-fifties, tall with auburn hair and dressed with the restrained elegance of a Parisian, she stood just ahead of me in line and we began to chat. Our shopping completed, Liliane invited me for chocolate at her favorite cafe opposite the Jardin du Luxembourg. Lugging our groceries up the steep hill, we settled into our chairs at an outdoor table and melded into a reunion of souls who had seemed to know each other since time immemorial. Oddly enough we hadn't yet formally exchanged names, and when she told me her name was Liliane, I felt a rush of fear—or was it excitement?—since Lilian was my mother's given name. We spent the next two hours in that cafe, sharing stories of our lives, our marriages and our children… our loves and our longings.

Stopping at a flower shop on the way back to Place Maubert, Liliane asked the florist to wrap up some flowers and then handed me an armful of bright yellow freesias. We hugged as we said goodbye, both of us knowing we would meet again. Inside the apartment, I put the freesias, which had not yet released their fragrance, into a vase on the marble mantelpiece and returned to the bedroom to rest. As I drifted into sleep, a slight perfume wafted over me and soon the air was alive with the flowers' heady fragrance. Enfolded in a happiness that was not of this world, I drifted back into the sleep of a child who had wandered upon an enchanted land, where everyone is a best beloved. Later, in the living room, I stood opposite the mantle looking at the freesias, perfect in color and design, but holding no hint of fragrance, as they had not yet opened. I didn't try to understand. I still have one of those delicate, yellow flowers, ever beautiful, tucked between the pages of my travel book.

That evening, to celebrate Jen's birthday, we walked across Place Maubert on our way to meet Cathy at Le Bar à Huîtres where we planned to dine. The Place hummed with expectation: lovers embraced under chestnut trees, families walked their familial pets, and students caroused in unquiet debate. On Boulevard Saint Germain, the traffic played its perpetual overture as commuters emerged from the Metro. Above the hubbub, I heard a voice calling, "Joan, Joan," and turning saw Liliane through the crowd.

She introduced Jennifer and me to her husband, Jean-Jacques, who murmured, "enchanté," and kissed my hand in the prescribed manner: a greeting I accepted with affective modesty. Chatting amicably, he conveyed his amazement at my meeting with Liliane earlier that morning. "C'est extraordinaire," he concluded.

"Extraordinaire," I agreed. Liliane and I hugged as though we had successfully choreographed a blessed event. And then we parted.

Toward the end of the week, weary from the heat and the humidity and all the walking, I sat in the little garden across the street from our apartment, reflecting on a host of converging emotions. I thought about my mother's pride in her French forebears and about the love that Jen and I share, the love that my mother and I could not. I thought about my father, a dispatch rider in France during WWI, riding his motorcycle through the filth and horror of Flanders. And all at once I sensed the longing that is with me whenever I visit France. It is a longing rooted in an unremembered epoch, as if some part of me belonged in France, a part that never belonged in England. And I thought about the enchantment that remained over my meeting with Liliane—a meeting without end.

On Friday, our last night, Jen and I boarded an excursion boat for one last cruise along the Seine. In the cool of that August evening, drifting along the river, my pulse relaxed into kaleidoscopic impressions of both the fleeting past and the beauty of a disappearing present. We cruised up to the Eiffel Tower, brilliantly claiming ownership of its sky, and back toward the venerable Ile de la Cité and Notre Dame, then around the Ile Saint Louis, whose illuminations shine more gently with the patina of each passing century. On the Left Bank, in a small park, several couples slow-danced to live music. Watching them as we floated past, I felt a longing for a time when I would have been out on the grass with them, dancing until midnight with my true love.

Mother and Daughter

You are not your children.
They are the sons and daughters of
Life's longing for itself.

Kahlil Gibran

I watched her every move, her every facial expression. And I never stopped watching the empty space of her absence. I firmly believed my mother was a witch. She would look accusingly into my eyes and tell me that she knew exactly what I was thinking, while I, unaware of my mind's wanderings, would obediently quiver under the weight of imposed guilt.

As a child, I walked with my mother to the grocery store in town and observed her looking around making sure that people knew she had arrived. My mother dressed enticingly for these outings, her clothes—which she made herself—adorned with sparkling costume jewelry, a glittering earring dangling from one ear. She greeted the shopkeeper with a disarming smile and a lingering gaze, as a prelude to placing her order. In England it was not the custom to choose one's own produce—the good apples along with the bad were handed over—so it was wise to maintain a cozy relationship with the shopkeeper.

Dining out with my father, she wore her favorite creation, a pink sequined gown along with a diamante necklace with matching bracelets. The sadder she felt the more brightly she dressed. My friends yearned for a mother as elegant as mine while

43

I yearned for a mother who was plump and ordinary, and who did not demand attention—particularly from men. Alongside my mother, I walked with my head down, feeling shy and embarrassed and inadequate, a dark shadow clinging to this bright flame. Without her it felt like death.

My mother was three years old when her mother died, and she and her two younger siblings were raised by their Victorian grandmother, in a household run with regimental exactitude, amidst the ever-present threat of a punitive God. She remembered her terror on awakening at nights to hear the ominous scratching on her bedroom door—a reminder she was told the following morning—of God's displeasure at her errant behavior. Later she learned that a housemaid had been instructed to play God so that my mother would know guilt. My mother told me that she never remembered being hugged or even held by her grandmother or by anyone. The last time I saw my mother, about a year before she died, she told me in a tremulous voice that her alcoholic father had done dreadful things to her when she was a child. As she spoke she closed her eyes and turned her head away, her body shrinking into a helpless acquiescence.

Trained as a singer, my mother's mezzo-soprano rang out with the stridency of a clarion call to arms. The few times we went to church I can still hear her, all five feet five inches with her auburn hair and elegant attire, standing tall as if on stage, belting out a hymn. Her powerful voice was a signal for the congregation momentarily to escape the service and to search for the voice. Next to her, I would blush with the shame of recognition and wish I could vanish under the pew. But my mother sang on undaunted, gathering steam with each verse. She was a natural actress who hid her vulnerable self beneath the roles she played in her daily life. It was rare that I was allowed a glimpse inside her impenetrable fortress. Six years old, I was sitting at our kitchen table, watching her slice onions into a bowl as tears began to fall among the onions. Glancing up at my mother, I saw the unthinkable: she was shaking with sobs. I had never seen my mother cry; in our home tears were severely discouraged since they implied a weakness of character. I rushed to console her, but she pushed me aside angrily, asserting that they were indeed onion-tears, and told me to hasten out of the kitchen. We both knew they were mother-tears, and I retreated into my room and cried for our mutual unhappiness.

Of Irish and French descent, she was lively, amusing, seductive—I lost at least one boyfriend to her charms—and she had a middle-class grit and determination that seemed to have been inbred, perhaps as protection against the all-too-eager judgment of others. My mother's own deference to the class system extended to the anti-Semitism prevalent in England at that time. The English were trained to queue and many times she would jostle her way to the front of the line, dragging me by the hand, *to get ahead of that Jew.*

I remember her dealings with our young Irish maids who often arrived at our house penniless. Grossly underpaid, they worked more than twelve hours a day only to be dismissed for the slightest infraction. On one such occasion, I stood by our front door, an unwitting accomplice to my mother's cruelty, as she inspected a weeping girl's belongings, to be sure our silver didn't go out into the night with her. I don't think that seventeen year-old knew a soul in London.

My mother was twenty years old when she married my father, their union precipitated by an unwanted pregnancy. My father was—according to my mother—the only person who had ever been kind to her. After a few years of marriage, however, she discovered that his kindness also extended to other women. Her disappointment and fury about my father's infidelities became the centerpiece of her life and, by extension, of mine and of my sister's. Doreen and I became the shock absorbers for our mother's grief and, as her lamentations flowed, so did our guilt. After our father had fled, there was no one else to blame. And each day, like mechanical marionettes, my mother and I (my sister wisely kept quiet) chanted an unvarying script: my mother, bitterly: "I gave up everything for you, my singing career—

everything." Me, sullen: "I didn't ask to be born, did I?" To which there was no logical answer.

There was no quiet in our house, only the voice of my mother intoning her grief like a phonograph needle stuck in a groove. It was as if the graveyard of her existence, every haunting memory—the death of her mother, her punishing childhood, the sexual abuse by her alcoholic father—had been resurrected and transformed into a crescendo of rage against my father's iniquities. Doreen and I were told that *he was a satanic man, and a sexual pervert who was probably infected with one of those diseases. A liar, a swindler and, worst of all, possibly a Jew.* We were told that our father had abandoned us, whom he had never loved, in favor of his women. My sister was especially vulnerable to my mother's ire. The product of that accidental pregnancy, Doreen had inherited our father's features and according to my mother, she had also inherited every one of our father's negative traits, a treasonable offense that my sister was never allowed to live down. I, on the other hand, looked more like my mother. She told me that I was her loved child and her only reason for living. It was a devouring and conditional love, however, and a seduction I encouraged with every atom of my being. There was an unspoken dichotomy in our household: on the one side were my mother and me, and on the other side my father and Doreen, whom he tended to protect during battles with our mother.

Even before my parents separated, I saw little of my father. He was out of the house early in the morning and gone until late in the evening. For me to cross party lines and get to know him would have taken more daring than I could muster, so I opted for the security of my mother, who was my sole source of survival. (I learned this early on, when she had a nervous breakdown and left for a few weeks of solace in the countryside. Though I was only eight-months old at the time, my sense of abandonment remains to this day.) Whenever my mother became overly stressed, she would threaten to leave us again as my father had done. I deliberately played a role that manipulated my mother into my camp, reacting to her most minute actions in a manner designed to win her undying love. We had entered into a Faustian pact: she would never leave me and I, in return, would give her my unqualified allegiance.

But whenever I listened to my mother's tirades against my father, I felt a mounting rage in my gut. I remained silent, however, fearing to tempt her displeasure. The one time I joined forces with Doreen and yelled at my mother, she turned her eyes heavenward and fainted. It took much pleading for us to revive her and when she decided to open her eyes, we were informed that our behavior would doubtlessly result in her imminent death. I don't think I ever yelled again.

When I was fifteen, the angers and resentments I had accumulated against my mother began to surface. My love for her moved underground, and all the muck of my unvoiced angers and resentments flowed like polluted waters between us. I hated her attitude toward my father whom she had always treated like a second-class citizen, her attitude toward men in general, her habit of inviting a seduction and then repulsing it with the vigor of an indignant virgin. I hated her anti-Semitic remarks and her attitude toward the lower classes. Caught between a mix of guilt and fear, I rebelled. I refused to go to school and, lying about my age, got a job at a department store in the West End. For forty hours a week, at low pay, I sat on a high stool in the basement of D. H. Evans of London and sewed tabs onto silk stockings. The work was automatic, so my mind was free to roam. It was my therapy and for the first time I began to meet myself having finally moved out of my mother's shadow. I never discussed my rage with my mother, since she would have defended her position by attacking mine and I was no match for her unremitting rage. So we continued our symbiotic inter-weavings, playing our prescribed roles in the only way we knew.

* * *

World War II broke out in 1939 and my mother moved out of London to the relative quiet of the countryside, so we saw little of each during the war years. I married Art in 1944 and left London for my new life in the United States. We had our two children; I loved and was loved, and I'd never known such happiness. Then inexplicably my happiness did a swift about-turn. Instead of joy, I knew only abject and persistent fear; pieces of my self became unglued from its moorings and the person I used to be slowly moved away, as if sucked into an unfathomable void. I longed for my mother, whom I had not seen for seven years, and I began to fantasize a reunion with her where our oppositional fences would burn and melt under the intensity of familial love. I imagined that she would, in some magical way, reassemble the puzzle of me. So Art and I invited her to visit for six weeks. For my mother and for me it was the most agonizing time we'd ever endured together. We both gave of our best, but neither of us could erase the indelible imprints of our ingrained patterns. I gave her no leeway. Every move she made in my house and with my children was a replay of myself as a child and all my furies rose up once again. Each day I sank lower and lower, and then one day after she'd been with us for about three weeks, things blew apart. My son Jonathan, was storming around the dining room having a six year-old tantrum, and I heard a familiar threat flowing like poison out of my mother's mouth. "You are a naughty little boy! Don't you know that you will make your mother ill with your behavior?" That evening I looked her in the eye and told her she had to go home, since it simply wasn't working out. It was the cruelest truth I'd ever spoken. I wrote her an explanatory letter hoping to ease her homecoming, but she wrote back telling me that I was obviously mentally deranged and in need of forgiveness.

* * *

I was fifty-six, the year before my mother's death, when I made the journey from my home in Berkeley, California, to see her

in Reading, about thirty miles west of London. As a result of
having Parkinson's disease, she was no longer ambulatory and had
to live in a private nursing facility. Here, she shared quarters with
four elderly women, all of whom were living in their own delusional
worlds. Walking into that dark cave of a room, I had difficulty
recognizing my once-elegant mother. She lay in a twin bed, in a
pool of urine that must have been there for days, as some of it had
seeped onto the floor. Her short, stylish hair, which had always
been tinted auburn, had turned dirty white and was long and
matted. She was old and frightened, and I was overwhelmed with
compassion for her. In our mutual vulnerability we reached out and
held onto each other.

Before I took her from that soulless place, I bought a box
of chocolates for her to offer to the other women in her room.
Immediately, though, my mother's child within rose up in outrage
and she found her old, audacious energy. With her mind still clear
amidst the pandemonium around her, she refused to give them a
single chocolate, saying they had been cruel to her. With much
clamor from the four women—they pleading, my mother with
intense pleasure, refusing—we left in an ambulance to move her to
a local hospital for rehabilitation.

On my last day in England, after we hugged goodbye, I
turned to wave to her one more time, and she managed to sit up
and give me one of her gutsy smiles. At the end of the ward, I could
not look back. I did not have her guts.

A year later, my mother telephoned to tell me that she was
ill and frightened, words I had never heard her use. I arranged to
fly over at once. By the time I arrived at the hospital, my mother
had had two strokes and had lapsed into a coma. Approaching her
bed in a ward of terminally ill women, I tried to blank out the
shock of seeing her, believing this had to be somebody else's
mother. Certainly not mine. I took her hand and whispered that I
was with her. At first there was no obvious recognition of my
presence, but then one tiny tear slipped through the widening
divide between us and trickled down her cheek. I reached for my

handkerchief to dab her face, but the tear had disappeared. I stayed a while in that ward of dying women, a few of whom were attached to drips or to pulsating machines, but were mostly left alone. The cubicles had no curtains and the place felt to me like a communal ingathering of souls embarking on their solitary journeys. The efficient young nurses changing the sheets on my mother's bed chatted amicably about their lives and their loves, while my inert mother protested their intrusion with a barely audible moan. I fought my urge to ask them to please include my mother in their conversation, since exclusion is hurtful and rude.

Later, as I left the building, one of those wild storms that occasionally appear in England blew in. Rounding the corner of the Intensive Care Unit, I was thrown to the ground by the wind. I sat there, unable to move, caught within an implacable emptiness, as if my identity, along with my mother's, was dissolving into that black turbulence.

That night, I awoke to a compelling smell, sweet and pungent, that hovered over the room like a broody cloud, permeating my skin and moving deep into my bones. I got out of bed and put my hands in a basin of warm water, thinking I could wash the smell away. But it persisted. The next morning at the hospital I learned that my mother had died at midnight, and I knew then that she had been with me to say goodbye. After signing next-of-kin documents, a nurse informed me that, according to custom, they had *laid out my mother* and did I wish to view her? I simply replied, *no.*

The cremation took place a couple of days later; the ashes were to be scattered around the roses of a tiny church near Reading. While my mother's son-in-law, her two grandsons, and I stood outside waiting for the minister to arrive, I noticed four men in tall black hats and long jackets carrying a coffin on their shoulders. One of the men motioned for us to follow them, and for a second I thought we were being asked to give our presence to an unknown soul on its way to the grave. As I walked across the lawn of the church, it was only then that I realized it was my mother inside that coffin. I wept for her lonely exit in that unforgiving box.

The men led us to our designated pew, and I sat and watched as my mother's coffin was positioned onto runners in front of the altar. After the minister made a few canonical pronouncements, a door nearby opened revealing the fire on the other side. The coffin moved slowly along its runners into the flames, and I had to close my eyes and put my hands over my mouth to stifle a scream. I felt I was being sucked out of my skin and into that fire with my mother.

Among my mother's belongings I found her favorite carriage clock, some jewelry, a few of my letters, and a small notebook in which she had written: *March 6, 1929, Bill left, and November 20, 1936, divorced Bill.* Recalling the cheerless day I'd spent with her when she was granted her divorce at the courthouse in Central London, I felt her deep lingering sorrow. Underneath all of her bitterness and rage, she had still loved my father.

Woven together by an invisible cord, which all but bound our souls, it was through my mother I learned about love and loss and survival. And as I remember our moving apart and our eventual coming back together, it all seems to have had a purpose. In an ironic way, she was my greatest teacher.

Widowhood

To every thing there is a season.

Ecclesiastes 3:1

Widowhood is not a many-splendored thing. Not initially, anyway. In the beginning there are endless documents to be read and understood and signed, official forms with their little black boxes inquiring into one's marital status. For almost fifty-two years I belonged in the married box. Now it's a different box I mark. The first time I checked the widowed box every past abandonment, real or imagined, rose up from the depths to invite me back. Diminished and demoted, I felt like an unloved, wrinkled rag hung on a line to dry.

A few years into widowhood, I make these official marks with less heartache and with a trace of defiance even, as if to challenge a doubting god. But I'm still shocked at my initial reaction. It jars me to think of myself acting as if I'd been disenfranchised when moved into the white space of that small box. Unhinged from my safe mooring, I no longer felt loved but like a woman fallen from grace and expelled from Eden. I ask myself if it takes a man to make a woman—an Adam to make an Eve—then remember that it was Eve who first ate that apple and Adam who followed.

Art's death has done strange things to my psyche. His

absence has unraveled my protective clothing, revealing deep secrets that were once so carefully incubated. At times I find myself afloat, vulnerable to every passing emotion, with all my once-confident answers withering into amorphous questions. It's like the outer layer of my skin has dropped off, leaving me naked with all of my frailties exposed. It seems the old status quo is gone forever and the newness of everything sits silently waiting to greet me. A reluctant joiner, I'd rather forget the whole widowhood thing and cling to a past whose substance dwells in memories. But memories, I know, require re-fueling from a living, vibrant present lest they fade and become dulled into petrified ash.

Around each corner of widowhood I find new challenges, hurdles attached to every event: the everyday ordinary of maintaining the house and the car, coping with the garden and a damaged watering system. Things once taken so lightly by Art I now approach with such hesitation. Even fear. Part of me is missing and I feel a chill that has nothing to do with the weather and everything to do with grief, this new companion of my days and nights. After Art's death, the first time I drove to the gas station I nervously studied the instructions on the pumps as if I was about to take a mid-term. But then I couldn't even unscrew the gasket to my gas tank. Humiliated, I drove to a nearby full-service station and did my homework, watching the attendant's every move. Turns out I had been turning the gasket in the wrong direction. Outside the bank on the busy corner of Solano Avenue, next to the stand where I buy flowers, I lingered an unusually long time, chatting with the flower man before facing the ATM machine, which rejected my card three times until I realized I'd omitted to punch in my personal identification number. When the new twenty-dollar bills slid effortlessly into my hands, my trembling ceased and I felt clever beyond belief.

Reflecting on the early days after Art's death, I remember my initial blessed numbness. I also remember my not-so-blessed sleeplessness. Grief intruded into my nights and interrupted my once-familiar dream patterns. For weeks I drifted in and out of light sleep at regular intervals. The moon illuminated the shelf above my bed, and I'd stare at the clock Art had designed, occasionally playing one of his C.D's. Unremembered dreams lingered just below the surface of consciousness, protecting me against an intrusion too awesome for my soul's assimilation. The first time I slept for more than two consecutive hours, I dreamt our closest friends, Don and Emily, had come to dinner at our house before going to a play. They had just returned from a trip abroad and I was telling them that Art had died. They responded with "Oh, he did?" and went on to tell me enthusiastic stories of their trip. Art's death and I were treated as non-events.

* * *

I think the isolation is what was most painful. Etched into my frozen aloneness, I believed there was nobody, not one person who knew what I was experiencing. Well-meaning, empathetic friends assured me otherwise, but how could they truly know how lost I felt without Art, without inhabiting my skin? I felt as if I was withering and drifting, a floating speck of unattached matter moving into hostile darkness.

Taking Art's clothes out of their familiar places was one of the most difficult decisions to make. I'm writing as though they were animate beings and, in a way, they were. His jackets and shirts and socks held the intimacy of his life, his living image, possessing the familiar shape not yet diminished by an absence of ownership. Art had great reluctance to wearing anything other than an old pair of patched pants and an equally worn-out jacket. Shopping trips had to be carefully orchestrated. I would find a jacket and suggest that it would look perfect on him, and this would be the signal for Art to counter with, "Just look at that price," or "It's not my color." Or in a more desperate tone, "But I've got two just like that at home." I'd plead with him that the jackets at home were twenty years old, the sleeves full of moth holes. At which point an alert salesperson would move us into a dressing room. With an enthusiastic push on my part, we'd buy the jacket and Art would wear it with a growing amount of well-hidden pleasure.

As I stood in the closet we once shared, touching Art's clothes, I remembered the occasions of their wearing: the light gray pants and white linen jacket he wore to the Carmel Bach Festival, the sweat pants he wore on our morning walks along the beach, the dark blue tweed jacket he wore to concerts at Zellerbach Hall, and his faded green corduroy jacket onto which I'd sewn brown elbow patches to hide the holes.

A few days after Art died, I moved one of his jackets over to my side of the closet. It was my favorite: a velour jacket with a front zipper that he had worn just a few days earlier. Soft and shapeless, devoted like a Newfoundland puppy, it was the one garment we had bought without any coercion on my part. Art had loved that jacket for over fifteen years, slid his fingers up and down the cool zipper, happy as a child with a security blanket.

I was going to leave those memories now, abandon them to the Collection Center of our local Salvation Army. Carefully I folded each garment as if to present priceless gifts to chosen friends. Then I packed all of Art's clothes into paper shopping bags and placed them in the back seat of my Honda.

Driving into the familiar parking lot on Solano Avenue, I found no one around. The staff who usually work the back door were all at lunch, so I left Art's clothes stacked against a gray, inhospitable wall. I drove through the Exit sign and then back again into the lot, repeating my route a few more times, as if my mind was directionless. The third time around I spun into action. I parked the car by the bags of Art's clothes, jumped out, grabbed the velour jacket into my arms and fled. I drove home, guided by instinct, a deluge from within keeping me from seeing the road. Back in the safety of my kitchen, I drank a stiff gin and tonic, though it could not obliterate the voice inside my heart that drummed out its message: *Art is dead.*

Doing double duty alone, though difficult, is not without its rewards. Life as a solo act brings with it certain freedoms.

Pushed to learn skills formerly not within my province, I am discovering, after the initial panic, a competency coupled with an unexpected exhilaration while I tackle my new world. Computers are not my worst enemy, I'm learning, as my keyboard and I are becoming cautious friends. A tentative plumber, I've repaired a defective toilet and fixed minor glitches in the garden watering system. Recently I even hammered an old garden fence back into shape. My most useful skill, though, is that of an efficient house manager who knows where to get help.

This sense of freedom bothers me, however, since it is accompanied by a tinge of guilt, an implied disloyalty to Art and to our marriage. It has nothing to do with our life together, I tell myself, in which I had the greatest of freedoms and the best of all worlds, but has more to do with an innate impetus that moves me to search for my own holy grail. Perhaps when sorrow confronts me in my empty places, I am forced to make a choice between the freedom to grow or the safety of remaining caught in the grayness of my despair.

In the Hospice bereavement groups I once led, I used to listen to the sorrows of others. I saw humanity at work and experienced the innate generosity of the human spirit. People of all persuasions joined together in the commonality of mourning the loss of a love. They offered their life's treasures—their stories—and I, still in my unruffled world, envied them their courage to trust. I hoped to touch them with understanding and with empathy, to help them in some way move through their heartaches into a new life. In those days, however, my head led my heart, since to over-identify with another's pain smudged the picture and obscured their path. There were times when holding someone whose sorrow overwhelmed me, I'd find myself wondering…what if this should happen to me?

Now that it is me who is living without Art, it is my heart I listen to. And I have begun to see many familiar patterns. The same basic responses to loss that I witnessed in those Hospice groups are now my emotions, tempered by my own experiences. It is the memory of those groups that nudges me out of my isolation into warmer waters. As I struggle to share my most intimate grief with the grief of another, my aloneness begins to melt and I see myself mirrored in the other. I recognize our essential oneness as I slowly become part of a We.

I do wish technology could keep up with death, however. There ought to be a 'Dead' button that removes the names of those who have died from the living rolls of potential donors to causes, worthy or otherwise. In the early days I couldn't bring myself to disclose to unknown corporate voices that Art had died. I dissembled and whispered that he wasn't in. Gradually, though, I've toughened up and now hear myself saying those fateful words.

One day last fall, around election time, an efficient voice called from Washington DC and asked for Art. Somewhat hesitatingly, I explained that he was no longer alive. The caller had been working two lines at once and there was a slight pause before the voice on the other end asked me when I would be expecting him back. Unable to answer, I hung up. Recently I received an invitation to a dinner addressed to both Art and me from an institution closely connected with Art, one which had sent me many supportive letters of condolence. Upon calling the office to remind them that Art was dead, I was informed with barely-concealed impatience that this was obviously a computer glitch. For those of us on the receiving end, however, such glitches are apt to freeze the blood.

I have learned a lot about attitudes toward death. Informing a voice on the phone that, "He is no longer living," or more explicitly, "He died," I have heard a myriad of responses. Some maintain their efficient tone while others reply that they will take him off their list or, casually, that they won't trouble me again. A few people react as though touched by some personal grief, and I find myself trying to console them. Still others simply gasp, mutter some incomprehensible sound and hang up. Some even say that they are sorry. In the end, I manage to have great sympathy for these voices. I don't think their training manuals touch on the subject of death.

Ultimately, though, death is part of all our Training Manuals. It is we who have to come to terms with accepting the unthinkable, the loss of a best beloved.

The Impresario

O Maiden hear. We love within us not one,
a promise, but all the zealous brew—not one
alone, but all the fathers reposing in us like
range upon range of decaying mountains...

Rainer Maria Rilke

Tall and skinny, with fair-hair and blue-eyes, my father could charm the carrion from a crow. We met when he came home on leave from France, during World War I. He was twenty-five years old and I was just four months. As a child, I knew my father through the eyes of my mother who complained unceasingly about his gambling, his infidelities, and his lower-class origins. I've had to wrestle with this image for years, to filter out what is not mine.

Images of my father invade my dreams: he's racing his motorcycle down a steep hill in Devonshire with me in the sidecar. The brakes fail and he grabs me as we plough into a haystack by the side of the road...I'm sitting by him on the sofa in the dining room, helping him memorize a part for a play he's producing—intrigued, and a little shy, I watch him slide into the playboy role of his character... At night under my blankets, I try to block out the sound of my father's sobs from down the hall, his gambling debts having at last caught up with him.

I wake with a sense of incompletion, a grief, a longing to know this first man I loved, a man who was kind, gregarious and smooth-tongued. I can still hear his soft, cockney voice and easy laugh, see his workmanlike hands that, to the distress of my mother, I inherited.

She once told me that my father had had a "Dickensian childhood." He'd never known his own father and, until his mother remarried, they had been horribly poor. According to my mother, he had been a child of the London streets, scrounging for food in rubbish bins. He didn't have much in the way of a formal education, though his mind was quick and observing. A consummate actor both on stage and off, my father could mimic the accent and manner of any class, from the winking, back-slapping "Pleased-ta-meetcha" to the impeccably cool, hand-extended drawl, "How do you do."

During World War I, he and my mother performed for troops home on leave—my father at the piano, my mother singing. He ran a local drama group in Bloomsbury, and I still remember a play about a murderer on the rampage at an old country estate. Searching for the missing owner and supposed victim, the police entered the sitting room and discovered my father, bound and gagged, inside the grandfather clock.

"Daddy!" I screamed, running down the aisle, intent upon rescuing him. My father's stepfather owned a chain of successful butcher shops and took my father into his business. My father's shop was on Kentish Town Road, a few miles north of the center of London. The shop stood between the police station and a bakery, and across the street from a pub and a fish-and-chips shop. In defiance of strict parental rules, Doreen and I would buy three penny's worth of deep-fried potatoes and eat them out of soggy newspaper wrappings.

It was my father's custom to auction off the unsold meat at the end of each week. Late one Saturday night my mother took me to the shop, where a large crowd had gathered. Dressed in his white apron, my father stood in the street, holding up joints of beef, legs of lamb, pork chops, and strings of sausages. It was a circus-like occasion, and I'm still imprinted with the delight of standing by my mother, watching my father perform. Though my mother was forever ashamed of having married into "the trade," the reclaimed part of me knows how proud I was of my father as he stood there immersed in the role of ebullient ringmaster.

But I don't think my father ever felt a deep sense of self-acceptance. Having been so underprivileged, he made it his goal to be wealthy. He believed that money equaled acceptance, and he developed an addiction to gambling. There were times when we lived in relative luxury, complete with a blue Austin car that Doreen and I would scrunch ourselves into during drives through the country. My father was happiest when driving, smoke from his Turkish cigarettes wafting into the back seat. Today when I smell a pungent cigarette or cigar, I sniff the breeze animal-like. In our more affluent times, we had a live-in housekeeper. During these times, my mother was less distraught and kinder to my father. At one point my father found us a housekeeper named Mrs. Donaldson who moved in with her five-year-old son, Christopher. An attractive, competent woman in her mid-thirties, she had been recommended, my father assured us, by one of his customers. The boy, however, had an uncanny resemblance to my father and it wasn't long before my mother's warning flags lit up. Another drama unfolded behind closed doors and Mrs. Donaldson and Christopher vanished from our house.

The good times were inevitably followed by the bad. The Austin disappeared, as did our household help, and my mother accused my father of gambling away his money, which he resolutely denied. One afternoon, Doreen and I were told by our mother to open our little metal money banks and hand over our sixpences and shillings to our father. I can still feel how sad I was for my father in his humiliation, still hear my mother's indignant voice: "He even took the children's savings."

And I remember some of my father's liaisons. There was Dulcie, the wife of a local doctor. The doctor decided to name my father in his divorce suit, but my mother intervened and the matter was quietly dropped. There was Marjorie, the cashier in my father's shop, who was quiet and shy, with dark hair and warm eyes. Marjorie's place was taken by Betty of the bold brown eyes and long red hair, who was neither quiet nor shy. I sensed these women's roles in our family's life and in an odd, conflicted way, I was happy for my father. In retrospect, I can see how disarmingly well my father played his role of the gentle charmer and how difficult life must have been for my mother.

I was twelve years old the day my father left the house for good. I returned home from school to an empty flat. The housekeeper was out, my mother had disappeared, and I had to wait outside until Doreen came home with the key. Opening the door to my room, I found that my bed, wardrobe, and chest of drawers were missing. For an instant, I thought I'd opened the wrong door until I saw my clothes in neat little stacks on the floor. In my parent's bedroom I found a note by the telephone from my father asking Doreen and me to call him. This is how we learned that he was not coming back. I knew then that he had taken my furniture, and I felt a twinge of hope that this might in some way hold him to me. When I asked if we would ever see him again, he assured me that we were his "darling girls" and that he would always be there for us. Not until many years later did I feel the abandonment and despair of that moment.

Though I occasionally saw my father for tea after he left, I rarely saw him alone. Betty, his current interest, was ever present, and I slipped into the role of mute observer during the few times I went to visit him. Once, calling on him unannounced, I climbed the stairs to his flat above the butcher shop and was startled when he rushed out and blocked my path. Having obviously disturbed a tryst, I waited, embarrassed, on the landing with my father before going up. Inside, Betty sat drinking tea. Thirteen years old, and on the cusp of my own sexuality, I blushed for the three of us. After that, I never visited my father's flat again.

My mother, Doreen, and I remained in our flat in Highgate, north of Kentish Town for a few more months and then moved to North Harrow, about an hour's train ride away. After a year,

Doreen—who quarreled constantly with my mother—moved closer to my father, and our family was split into two camps. Over the next few years I saw little of my sister or my father. Though he would occasionally take me to a movie, I was uneasy whenever I was with him, as if I were indulging in a forbidden adventure.

I was sixteen when my father phoned to tell me about a job he thought I would like, working with the registrar of a well-known South African gold mining company. He'd heard about the job from one of his women friends. It had been more than two years since I'd seen my father, and I took his unexpected interest in my life to be a loving act. My mother, meanwhile, was scathing in her criticism of my having anything to do with one of my father's women. The job turned out to be a steppingstone toward my dream of working in Europe. I like to believe that my father was pushing a little against that door I had tried to close between us.

For the next few years, my father and I made no effort to communicate. From Doreen I learned that he was managing a hotel in Surrey, south of London. Then World War II broke out, and for the next four years I was wholly engaged in my own life. After Art and I were engaged, however, I decided I needed my father to meet the American I was to marry. Doreen gave me my father's new address, so I wrote to him. He replied promptly, and invited me to spend a few days with him and his wife, Dorothy. It was a meeting in which we never quite met. My father was his usual pleasing self, but there was an emptiness between us that felt like a still, dark cave, into which neither of us were willing to venture. Instead, we circled each other like fencers, resolutely sticking to the rules of the game. It was then I realized that as a child I had never really known my father. I had always been perplexed by his artful, glib phrases, which flowed like scripted cues but seemed to lack genuine feeling. And I recalled his deft placating of my mother, whom he called his "queen," despite their troubled relationship, and of my sister and I who were forever his "darling girls."

The night before I was to end my visit with my father and Dorothy, they took me to the local pub for dinner. Watching my father take on the role of convivial host, I found myself wanting to tell him that he no longer needed to play-act. Instead, I withdrew into my old silence, and when Art arrived to pick me up I was close to tears. The four of us spoke the perfunctory language of avoidance; Art, who was not very good at small talk, did his best to be at ease around this broken family. Saying goodbye to my father that night, he told me that he thought Art was "a good chap." A few weeks later, Art and I were married and left for the States.

I was forty years old when Art and I returned to England with our two children, Jonathan and Jennifer. Art was on sabbatical from the University of California, Berkeley, and we'd rented a house in Cambridge. After three months in England, though, I was beginning to fall back into my old childhood panic of feeling alone and abandoned. It had been fifteen years since I'd talked with my father, and I had an overwhelming urge to see him. So one windy summer day, Art and I drove with the children south to Brighton in a Studebaker we had brought with us from California.

At one point during our visit, I was immobilized with stomach pains. (Later, while traveling in France, I would have a second attack, and would learn that it was caused by an ailing gall bladder.) While Art and the children took a walk on Brighton Beach, my father and I stayed back at home. Curled on my father's bed, I reverted to that whimpering child who had been terrified of witch-mothers, the child who had lost her first love too soon. Holding my hand until I was quiet, my father was near tears himself. "Perhaps I should never have left you," he said. It was the closest moment we had ever had.

For a few years after that visit, my father and I corresponded in a sporadic manner. Each time an envelope with his graceful handwriting arrived, I would open it with wishful expectancy. While I longed for authenticity, though, his notes offered only smooth platitudes, and soon our letters petered out like embers in an un-stoked fire.

In 1974 Art and I visited England again. This time we stayed with Doreen in Uxbridge, north of London, for a few days and I spent some time with my mother who had fallen ill. It had been over sixteen years since I'd seen my father. Caught yet again between longing and disappointment, I debated whether or not to call him. Doreen, impatient with my indecisiveness, dialed our father's number and handed me the phone. Hearing his lilting accent, I felt a twinge of my old distrust. Yet at the same instant, I knew that I needed to see him. Art and I arranged to drive over for tea the following afternoon.

Greeting us at the door of his small cottage, my father was dressed for the occasion in a brown suit complete with waistcoat and tie. "Hello my darling girl," he said, hugging me, and I felt as if the sun itself were warming my heart. While Dorothy made our tea, my father led me into the garden to pick some lettuces, and it was here he asked about my mother, something he had never done. When I told him how ill she was, he only said, "Poor old girl," and looked away. Then he added, "She was quite naughty, you know." I didn't comment, and he didn't expect me to. Looking into my eyes, he said, "You have a smile just like your mother's." Startled, I blushed as though I had just received my first valentine.

Two years later, my brother-in-law, Reg, called me from London to say that my father was seriously ill. Reluctant to elaborate, he insisted only that I would not want to see my father in his current state and assured me he'd call again soon. That night I had visions of my father—chain-smoking, riding his motorbike, acting up there on stage, ever jaunty in his walk—a man who had reached for dreams he never quite caught and who was now lying in a hospital bed, his every breath a struggle.

I had a job interview with a counseling agency in Oakland the following morning, and as I was leaving the house I heard the telephone ring. Somehow I knew it was the call from London to say that my father had died. But I closed the door behind me, hurried down the steps to the car and drove into the day.

Art's death has done strange things to my psyche. His absence has unraveled my protective clothing, revealing deep.

The Collector

Who, if I cried out, would heed me
amid the host of the angels?

Rainer Maria Rilke

"Help," I called to the man in the toll booth. "I went the wrong way."

Ulla, Marta and I were about to celebrate my eightieth birthday the way we always celebrate our birthdays, with lunch on Cronkhite Beach, nestled at the base of the Marin Headlands. Ulla was supposed to watch for our exit off the highway just before the Golden Gate Bridge. Once missed, however, there was no exit. Forced to cross that bridge, we had no choice but to stop at the toll plaza.

"That'll be $3.00," the man announced.

"But I don't want to go into San Francisco. I need to turn around." By now I was pleading.

"Three dollars," he repeated.

Highway One is a commuter's route flowing from the untamed beaches and hamlets of Marin's incomparable beauty into San Francisco's crooked streets. Traffic at lunchtime is heavy with all lanes open and drivers flashing by waving pre-paid passes or stopping to pay cash. There I sat, panicked at the thought of plunging into that foggy city where I was sure we'd be lost forever.

Cars kept piling up behind us. I braced myself for road rage. But there was none. Instead, our lane settled into a benign quietude as if to herald the beginning of the day's featured film, while in the lanes on either side of us the speeding traffic continued its hungry flight.

I handed over the three dollars.

The man in the tollbooth opened his door and stood alongside my car.

"Where are you from?" he asked.

"From England," I replied, staring straight ahead.

"That's not good enough," he said. "Where in England?"

"London," I answered with singular docility.

"How about Hampstead/Highgate?" he ventured.

I told him he was exactly right. It was then I knew that he and I were fellow sojourners on enchanted ground. Through the years, whenever friends have asked where I come from, I have always told them Hampstead/Highgate, a name I coined to describe the area a few miles north of London, where the town of Highgate segues into Hampstead Heath.

Oblivious to the cars in the line behind me and to Ulla and Marta in the car with me, I continued to stare straight ahead, unable still to gaze upon the face of this stranger. He bent closer to my window and said in a matter-of-fact tone, "Guy Fawkes wasn't guilty, you know."

I carefully considered his statement as if we'd been in the midst of discussing English history. In 1605, in retaliation against the persecution of English Catholics, Guy Fawkes and his co-conspirators had tried to blow up Parliament and King James I.

"No," I replied, "Perhaps he wasn't." In the silence that followed, neither of us made a move, our conversation hovering. I hadn't thought about Guy Fawkes since I left England where, every November 5th, Guy Fawkes Day is celebrated with families gathering to light huge bonfires and set off firecrackers. But now I could think of nothing else. I wanted to stay in my car, in this place, and grasp this moment so that it couldn't escape.

But as the spell began to fade, I found I was back in my

agitated mode. Marta, who was sitting next to me, asked what was going on and I replied that I honestly didn't know. Ulla, in the back, equally uninformed, told me to tell that guy to get us off the bridge.

He didn't need to be asked. He pointed to an unmarked passage just beyond the toll plaza. He told me to turn right, continue through the underground tunnel, and keep going until we hit the road back. Highway patrol cars and tow trucks loomed haphazardly in our path and then, barely discernible in the gloom, there was a sign giving us a choice of direction: south, to the city— or north, back towards our beach. This time we paid attention.

As we emerged from the tunnel the sun had never appeared more radiant. Marta and Ulla asked me again what that conversation had been about, and I replied that I was as confused as they were. What I didn't tell them as we drove up the steep hill to the Headlands, and down the long winding road to the ocean, was that I was dazzled with an excitement and a joy so compelling that I wanted to open all the car windows and shout a greeting to every passing driver. I wanted to embrace every stranger, everywhere. It was a moment of invincibility, as if I'd been handed a free pass to a utopia of my own design, where nothing was beyond my reach.

It was low tide as we walked through the shifting sands toward our usual picnic spot, where we could see the bridge above the Pacific Ocean, glowing like a victorious Athena, as it danced a stately gavotte with the wind. The sun, the sand, the wind, typically leave me dragging my feet as I transmogrify into a beach slouch, but on this day the very elements gentled my path and I drifted along with the buoyancy of a child whose heart is not yet tarnished.

Gathered under the cliffs, I was startled to find a dozen women friends waiting to celebrate with me. Had I known in advance that anyone besides Marta and Ulla would be there, I might have sequestered myself at home, as I am shy at being the focus of attention. But the element of surprise disarmed me, and the afternoon turned into a carnival of delight. A delight not only engendered by the familiar wild seascape, but a delight in being with women I both admire and love.

On our way back to Berkeley, Marta, Ulla and I settled into our individual silences, satiated with the friendship, the food, and the champagne. Driving with the flow of homebound traffic, I clung to the glow that had filled my day. A true believer in the Buddhist ideal of surrender, I sometimes falter when it comes to actual practice. I had no intention of letting go of the warm reception I'd just received; it was already engraved in my mind to be remembered in moments of low self-esteem. Neither could I let go of the haunting familiarity of that toll collector. How did he know exactly where in London I'd grown up, and what did his cryptic statement about Guy Fawkes mean? Why had I been unable to look him in the eye? Though I had no logical answers, I sensed that some part of me had received a message and that, in due time, it would translate itself.

Later that evening when Ulla called to talk about my conversation with "that man," and suggested that we drive back to the bridge the next day and check him out, I was close to tears. I told her I couldn't talk about it right then and we said goodnight. I knew, though, that I would not retrace my steps, since I couldn't bear to discover the magic of the day was merely the invention of a deluded imagination.

The middle of the night is my witching time, when remnants from the day's disorder float up like unheard children to remind me of our inescapable affinity. A lucent sliver of moonlight, outlining the redwood trees that dwell like sentinels in the park across the road, caught my eyes as I emerged from sleep. Simultaneously, the motion detector in the garden flooded my bedroom with light. Fully awake now, and not a little agitated, I stood at the window to find a deer dining on my camellias. The tawny, sloe-eyed buck raised his antlered head and we gazed at each other, unblinking and in silent communion for a full minute. Then, confident of his territorial rights, he resumed his meal and I walked upstairs to brew myself a cup of tea.

At two o'clock in the morning, the taste of peppermint tea with a touch of honey is kin to mother's milk in its hypnotic soothing of the senses. I sat at the dining room table, my hands stroking the warm mug, and ruminated over the events of my birthday. My mind kept probing for logical answers to imponderable questions. Back in bed two hours later, and bereft of an answer—how could logic deal with the illogical?—I warmed into sleep and caught a passing thought about my father who had fled our family home when I was twelve.

The clatter of the garbage collector tossing my recyclable cans and bottles into the city's omnivorous truck outside my window broke my sleep and, in that moment between night and day, my inner, oracular voice told me that the man on the bridge was, in some unfathomable way, my father reaching out to me. As I lay there reflecting on the interweaving events, it all seemed eminently clear to me. I've always believed that there is no chasm between life and death, only kindred souls that travel between these two realities as along the continuum of a shining Moebius strip. For more than half a century, I've wrestled with my relationship to my father and have engaged in countless celestial conversations, in which we listened to each other's divergent memories, so that I meet him now through less biased eyes.

Guy Fawkes wasn't guilty, you know, played over and over in my head during the following week, like the lament of an unrequited lover. What was the link between that fifteenth-century insurgent and my philandering twentieth-century father? I continued to worry the question, then waited until the muddied became crystalline. Quite suddenly, early one morning in the quietude of my studio, I understood. Both of these men had been accused of attempting to destroy houses—literally in the case of Guy Fawkes, and figuratively in the case of my father who had abandoned our fractured family. Guy Fawkes had paid with his life, my father paid with a blistered guilt, not lessened by my mother's inconsolable, all-encompassing rage.

This was the only time my father had ever pleaded his case to me, and I took his parental olive branch firmly in both hands as if I'd been newly anointed. Closing my eyes for a moment, I replayed my initial meeting on the bridge with the toll collector. This time, just as our conversation was ending, I took off my dark sunglasses, moved out of my car and joined him, unattended by doubt. "Hello Daddy," I said, looking directly into his eyes. "I knew you would come."

"It's been a long time, hasn't it," he replied.

"Yes," I agreed, "it has."

Touching my shoulder lightly with his hand, my father continued. "But then time…time is forever, is it not?"

As the rising sun filtered through my window, I sat and thought about angels who, defying logic, appear in unexpected places with unfamiliar faces—some of whom we recognize deep in our intuitive bones. Others unseen by our disbelief, simply meld into an attendant waiting until we, like hosts at a family gathering, open the door and invite them in.

Love Is a Four-Letter Word

In this world of love
We are the hidden treasure,
We are the owners of eternity.

Rumi

My friend Julie telephones me once a month from her home in New York. She talks about her work, her children, her husband, her longed-for-lover, and her hope that I'm surviving. Before hanging up, she says, "Bye. Love you." "Love you, too," I reply. But last weekend after Julie called, I remained troubled by the echo of my voice and catch myself now, in sundry conversations, indiscriminately tossing off "Love yous," with the studied intimacy of a telemarketer. It is a routine that does not persuade my heart. It is love that is misbegotten.

* * *

The matter of love continues to lodge in my mind like an unwelcomed tenant who defies eviction. Nudged into a dialogue with my inner censor, I seek to defend my facile use of so intangible a word. Love has become my mantra, my topic of conversation with close friends and, in fact, with anybody who will listen. To my surprise few people turn me down, or treat my compulsion as one more facet of advancing age. It turns out that nobody really knows how to define love.

We ardently declare that we love our spouse, our children, our extended families. We do not speak, however, of our declaration's whispered reminder that, on occasion, a base impulse to throttle them underlies our domestic felicity. Overwhelmed with guilt, we hastily reaffirm our invariable love. Love, it appears, is a four-letter word that, at times, ameliorates our darker instincts and enables us to redeem our expected sense of civility.

Before Art died, he told me that he would never leave me and he never has. Co-existing within illimitable space, he still walks beside me, permeating the given air I breathe. The shadowed touch of his hand is still with me in the shivering fog, in the warmth of the sun, in the deep, quiet of night as I continue to watch the evolution of our love.

We used to think that we were transparent in our togetherness, that our love was immutable, inviolate. But we were wrong. Interweaving across our singular realities we see each other now in a new and different way. It is as if we've slipped through the membrane of our restrictive consciousness to reveal a freedom we had never known. Old connubial compromises with lingering traces of resentment, anger, and doubt have vanished into the dim recesses, together with our self-protective armature. Faced with the unencumbered heart, our love is more profound, more binding in death than it was in life.

* * *

Dining at my friend Seth's house, he unexpectedly asks if I love him. Lulled by the sybaritic delights of food and wine and no less by our mutual embracing, I hesitate for a second. "Yes," I reply. "In a way, I do. And you?" I counter, instantly regretting my demand for a quid pro quo, since, according to Seth, the concept of love is a totally fraudulent conceit. In a barely audible voice, he tells me that, yes, he loves me.

Later, at home, alone in bed, I'm uneasy about my quick, albeit equivocal affirmation of love. Was my response embroidered by the exuberance of the moment, and is my feeling simply one of gratitude to Seth for his companionship since Art's death? Yet an urge to solace his soul, to pleasure him, flows unreservedly from a need deep inside of me; a need where sex is but a peripheral element floating around the center. When I am with Seth, I'm filled with an uncommon joy, as if a past love has been liberated and we are together again, dancing a sacrament of renewal.

At times, images of past loves haunt my recognition. Some, like perfumed apples sweet on the tree, I harvest with infinite tenderness; others, rank and bruised with disillusion, I long to forget. Fifteen years old, I am having supper at the home of Peggy, my best friend. Her brother Ron, an impressive four years older than I, offers to walk me home across the darkened park. He pauses at the base of a spreading oak tree and tells me to look up at the moon. I look up and on the coming down meet his eager mouth. My first kiss. Traumatized with shyness and guilt, and intrigued with the tantalizing feelings my body is experiencing, I gaze once again at the moon. Back home, I fantasize endless love and, surely a wedding. For Ron, however, it becomes an event that never happened.

In my later teens love was the expected Saturday night endearment. Packed into the half-priced balcony of our local movie theater, we teenagers experienced the thrall of hearing I love you waft off the screen and into our waiting ears, to be followed, we hoped, by a modest approximation from our less tutored escorts. Back then, my fantasies were indelibly colored in the idiom of love, and I would have handed over everything I owned, except my terrified virginity, to be courted by a willing Adonis.

By the time I was twenty, I had found Adonises of all ages and of all dispositions. A few lasted a week or so, but most turned into more enduring relationships, where I tasted the ecstatic relief of acceptance, mixed with the guilty pleasures of restrained sex. The idea of love was ever present, but its felt emotions were nowhere to be seen. I held them firmly chained in my underworld of disbelief.

* * *

In the chaos of World War II when I met and married Art, the gods were kind to me, since I had no wish to question the whereabouts of my emotions and obediently followed the call of my heart. It would take a few years' work before I would retrieve the ingredients of trust and courage, and the pain of ultimate loss, without which love is only an interlude that pleasures the moment, but lacks the enduring patina of beauty.

The biblical injunction to love thy father and thy mother scatters its seeds in the garden of our beginnings. An a priori love, filtered through our genes, it arrives with its palette bespattered with various hues, and is the ground of our being. It is the container of all other love and, for me, it conditioned my every faltering step. As a child, love was an emotion rarely expressed, its place overshadowed by a prevailing despair that evoked dark images heavy with mistrust. Yet I don't think love ever gives up. It waits, with Job-like patience, for us to deconstruct our imposed images, one by one, down to bare skin-essence, to the place of our belonging.

Images from the past, however, never fade completely. In subtle ways they inhabit my days, reminding me that moments of perfection contain their counterpoints. Days when, touched by a passing joy, the hours and I float together in soft contentment, and I'm lulled into believing that I'm everybody's best-beloved. There are also the days when I awaken with a brooding, fearful sense that there is no love out there, only a dark pit of emptiness, and anyway, who would love me? If I've done my homework though, I recognize the genesis of this theme and am able to placate my fears. But sometimes the enemy is more tenacious and clings in ways new to me, and I forget who I am. Later, walking in the park, I meet a friend who, with a simple word, gives me back to me.

* * *

For sixty years I have been a practicing parent. It is a journey rife with pitfalls, which, all too often, I fail to circumvent.

My deep longing to bring to my two children a love that is unconditional and steadfast is, at times, overlaid by an ingrained need to control the incertitude of their days. Familial love engages the emotions in a cornucopia of indelible sweetness and guilty disappointments, and my family is no exception. While we fulfill our roles with noble intentions, the path to our hearts can become littered with the debris of denial, as we lose sight of each other. With my son, I chose not to recognize his reservoir of rage that dwelt beneath a resigned compliance with the official status quo, and I was all too eager to protect my shy, clinging daughter from knowledge of her own strengths. Over the years, though, we have had to learn the art of authenticity, and there lives between us now a more honest love that may, on occasion, drift off course, but which instinctively returns to center.

* * *

On Berkeley's Sproul Plaza, I watch a white-haired street person, enshrouded in a faded caftan, move through the crush of emerging students chanting an inaudible song, as he holds high a sign that reads: THOU SHALT LOVE THY NEIGHBOR AS THYSELF. In the noontime cacophony of drumming and banging gongs, he maintains his unerring path, oblivious of all else but his happy compulsion. Sitting on a bench, awaiting a friend for lunch, I have an urge to ask him how he goes about loving his neighbors. But I am shy of intruding upon his journey and remain ever the observer.

The mandate to love my neighbor is a perfectly rational assumption. But is it not equally rational to feel anger toward a neighbor who cuts down my favorite fifty-foot bamboo to enlighten his garden? My daughter, Jennifer, a Buddhist by nature, might be annoyed, even disappointed, but she offers her compassionate love since she views his actions as those of an unloved child who grabs for fear of asking. I try to emulate

Jennifer, whom I admire beyond all women, but, unlike her, I'm not yet free of an expectant reciprocity on the scales of love.

* * *

During one of my spurts of self-education, I stumble through Milton's "Paradise Lost." Many of his allusions are beyond my thinking, yet day after day I live the story as if the personae are parts of myself. The host of good and bad angels, with their crisis of conscience, are not unfamiliar to my own wayward emotions. And with the wishful thinking of an innocent, I somehow translate Milton's epic, about the origin of evil, into an epic about the origin of love. For me this is a poem entirely about love, about the joining of Adam with Eve, about the courage to dare.

I believe this story is tucked into my genes, together with an observant Self who lives in the deepest part of my being; a Self who is mother to all my other selves who sometimes lose their bearings in a dispassionate world. And when I touch these depths, my doubts about the meaning of love vanish and the answer seems to have always been here. Love is the very planet in which we exist. It is the sun, the rain, the winds, the heavens and the good earth. It is consummate. And what we do with it is the story of our journey.

Coming of Age in Wartime

Love comforteth like sunshine after rain...

William Shakespeare

In the fall of 1938, I turned twenty-one and left London to live in Switzerland. This was the year I drove my cousin's motorbike smack into a tree, danced in an all-night marathon, and learned about a Nazi named Adolf Hitler. It was also the year I broke off my first affair.

I'd fallen into an uneasy liaison with a man who was more than twice my age. We were drawn together; he for his reasons, and I clearly (with hindsight) was in pursuit of a father figure. A new partner in a land development company, Stuart had requested a personal secretary and I, a fledgling typist, was presented to him as a possibility. We shook hands and he pulled up a chair for me in the corner of a large room. Cluttered with filing cabinets and desks and office workers, and a telephone switchboard operator chatting non-stop, the room quivered with disquietude. Apologizing for our cramped quarters—his own office for some reason unavailable—Stuart asked the few canonical questions about my background and experience, his encouraging smile soothing my in-house adversary who kept proclaiming my clothes dowdy, my hair bedraggled, my intelligence missing. "When can you come?" Stuart asked. I moved into his office the very next day.

A few weeks later he took me to lunch. Over appetizers he spoke about his years as a mining engineer in South Africa and in Europe. By dessert, I knew all about his marriage in which he and his wife, Amy, lived together in platonic amicability, indulging their separate affairs while their two children were away at boarding school.

I told him about Charles, the engineering student I was dating, who had recently taken me home to meet his Welsh parents. Dedicated Methodists, they did not welcome an infidel as a possible daughter-in-law, especially one whose parents were divorced. Charles, though, remained ardent and I thought I did, too.

In the popular pub atop Hampstead Heath, I was intrigued by Stuart's cosmopolitan background, his sharp mind and ready wit, which I hastened to match. I also luxuriated in the seduction of his unwavering interest. By our second lunch, I thought about my nightly telephone calls from Charles who, taciturn by nature, would lapse into broody patches of sighs and silences. No longer the gentle listener, I admitted to a certain boredom.

One afternoon over lunch, Stuart offered to teach me to drive the company car and, noticing my persistent cough, recommended I consult his doctor. Would I mind if he arranged an appointment? I had become a priority. In his car on our way back to the office, his hand rested on my arm for a brief, quiet moment, and I felt an attraction like magnet to steel. I knew there was danger there, and I plunged in as if my life depended upon it.

My first lesson in the two-door Studebaker embodied a mixture of nervous concentration and a heightened awareness of Stuart's over-eager solicitude. His arm around my shoulder had aims other than attending to the gears. In the encroaching darkness my body responded to his hand, and I blushed with the pull of my longings. Later that evening I angrily told him I'd have no more driving lessons. But the next evening I went back.

After I passed my driving test, Stuart and I continued to spend time together. Our working days sometimes extended into dinners, the theater and occasional weekend drives into the country. Charles, by now in vehement agreement with his parents about my unsuitability, ended his telephone calls. And while I entered into other attachments, there was always Stuart close by, whom I clung onto like the string of worry beads I stroked each morning. He introduced me into his circle of friends, who embraced me with familial acceptance and I, in turn, introduced Stuart to my closest friends, who remained bewildered by my elderly connection. My mother, forty years old and lonely, found Stuart charming. Stifling her fears that I had inherited the dark morals of my father, she wondered if Stuart might produce a lonely friend for her.

Soon my relationship with Stuart infiltrated the protective barriers I'd erected around my sexuality. At once a shy, 18 year-old and an almost-woman, my conforming self still anxious to please, my femininity was bursting forth. Ready to explode, I was also confused and haunted by guilt, enmeshed in this forbidden joy. Yet I did not try to escape. It was, in retrospect, the playing-out of an old story—incest at a distance, unconsummated.

But I was not a happy Jezebel. Our sexual war games—Stuart's step-by-step confronting, and my tentative ground-giving's—were always followed by an avalanche of tears. I was left feeling increasingly restive and sullied and knew that if I lost my virginity, I'd lose my mind. So I kept both. And after three years, I began to withdraw from our entangled relationship.

The summer of 1938, while vacationing with my mother in Castagnolia, Switzerland, I heard that the local finishing-off school was looking for someone to teach English. On impulse, I applied and got the job. Hired to teach English, tennis and rowing, I was also to chaperone the students at their weekly visits to Vanenies, the classiest cafe in town, where they would learn the etiquette of drinking afternoon tea along with the requisite social chat. The school, in return, would teach me German and French, provide room and board, and pay me a small salary. I became a cross between an elitist governess and a den mother to fifteen young women, many of whom were Jewish and had been sent out of Germany by their parents, in anticipation of what was to become the Holocaust.

Madam Rumpell, who ran Montebello College, was also Jewish and, I suspect, acting as an entry point for escapees from Germany. There was a mystery about the place—visitors arrived in the middle of the night and we met them the next morning at breakfast, observing their anguish. None of us could imagine the magnitude of the evil to come. Meanwhile, life at Montebello continued its usual routine and that winter we all traveled to the Swiss Alps for a two-week skiing vacation. During the second week, Stuart arrived to be with me. At the station in Andermatt I watched him emerge from the ski train among a group of skiers; tall with iron-gray, curly hair and intense blue eyes, he smiled his wide engaging smile and a part of me fled back into that familiar joy.

I spent the following summer working at the League of Nations in Geneva, and by fall left Geneva for a job interview in Milan, intending to stay for a year. But with the immanency of war, British travelers were advised to return home immediately, so I switched plans and traveled north across France to Calais. The English Channel crossing was rough and noisy, the boat packed with returnees trying to quell anxieties in the midst of so many unknowns. In Dover, Stuart was waiting for me and as we hugged, I felt the relief of a prodigal returning home for absolution.

World War II broke out in September 1939. Staying temporarily at my grandparent's house in Hampton Court, southwest of London, I spent my first weekend sandbagging buildings against the expected air raids. I can still hear the inconsolable wailings of our sirens as enemy planes flew over the southeast coast. Later, I remember the first and most devastating fire bombing of London. I was driving home after work and got out of the car to look back at the city, the sky glowing an incandescent orange, all of London looking as if it was in flames. Like an inferno out of hell, my senses were stunned. It was as if everything that defined my existence was melting into those flames and soon I, too, would cease to exist.

As the war progressed, London became a city with a changed face and I saw Stuart less frequently. Parents and children were separated for the duration, many of the younger children evacuated into the country, some sent to the United States and to Canada. Businesses simply closed or moved their offices out of the city. Amidst the chaos of this uncertainty, it was difficult to find a job and I spent fruitless days traveling an hour by train to London looking for work. Disheartened, I consulted Stuart who remembered a friend who had recently joined the Ministry of Food, a governmental agency that sprung into action at the beginning of the war. A few days later, Stuart drove me to my arranged interview and I emerged with a job as personal assistant to the departmental director of finance.

As the air raids increased over London, the main part of the Ministry was evacuated to Colwyn Bay in North Wales where, until we found our own housing, we were billeted upon the local townspeople who were not altogether happy with the intrusion of uninvited guests. Here I rented a room in a friend's house high on a hill in this town of quietude, the surrounding rocky landscape covered with purple heather, its hills nestling the solitary family farms. Cycling up and down those hills, we strangers—many parted from our families—began to form a close-knit community. It was during my time in Colwyn Bay that I finally ended my attachment to Stuart.

One evening at a party, where I knew few people, I glanced around hoping to find somebody to save me. Across the room I noticed a tall, fair-haired man of around 40 who was smoking a cigarette and drinking a glass of Scotch. He had the look of a seasoned partygoer and was talking animatedly to some friends. There was an odd familiarity about this stranger that at first puzzled and then excited me, and I found myself moving over to him with a confidence propelled by instinct rather than by knowledge. When I reached him, he turned to me and said, "Hello there," as though he'd been expecting me. He told me his name and I told him mine, and then I noticed that he had the same deep blue eyes and inviting smile that I'd first found so compelling in Stuart. "Let me get you a drink," he offered, propelling me across the room to the bar, his voice seductive with the innate assurance of the British landed gentry: the same voice my father would conjure up when he wished to impress an audience. Later that evening, after more drinks, he took me to another party where we danced late into the night, and I knew I was, once again, courting trouble.

I lost no time in furthering my affair with Roland. In times of war, relationships are forged by different rules and improvise their own melodies, since they exist within an implied impermanence. Roland invited me to his hotel for drinks a couple of times and then, one evening, we drove a few miles out of Colwyn Bay to a country inn for dinner. Over several glasses of wine, he talked about his wife and children to whom he was devoted, and made explicit their priority in his life. I was comforted by his honesty, as I had no wish to compete. I simply wanted someone who assumed an interest in me and on whom I could depend.

During those war years, work was a constant, parties an adjunct at the end of each day and alcohol a blissful antidote to stress. Roland was a full time smoker and a full time drinker, and for over two years he engaged my heart and challenged my mind. We bicycled on the weekends, drank together, danced together and often dined with friends in London where a skeleton staff remained. And, while our relationship was tender and, in a sense loving, it was never freely sexual. I was hide-bound by my sexual fears, and Roland was conscience-bound to refrain from the ultimate intercourse. We made love like two cautious teenagers.

Spring of 1942, I became disenchanted with my hedonistic life and with what felt like a troubling repetition of my amenable girlfriend role. Something was missing in the secure countryside of North Wales, and it was time for me to return to London. During one of my visits to London, a friend told me about a job opening with the American Embassy and suggested I apply. I did and was hired as secretary to the Head of the London Mission of the Office of Scientific Research and Development. Within a week I was back in London and soon, by unspoken agreement, Roland and I moved away from each other and into other relationships.

The war accelerated, London settled into the rhythm of a

city under siege, and I (together with everyone else) went about my business playing a kind of Russian Roulette with the bombs. The raids were particularly heavy in the morning when I was rushing to work, again at lunchtime, and then especially aggressive at night. And though I prided myself on being impervious to fear, an attending panic occasionally found its way through the cracks. Late one afternoon, in my office on the 8th floor of a building in the West End, I stood mesmerized, watching a bomb coasting along outside our window. I was taking notes from my boss, a man of measured invincibility whose emotions, if any, were firmly under wraps for the duration. Shaking with fear, my stomach plummeted to the ground floor. "You have a problem?" he asked. "Not at all," I managed to gasp, praying that the bomb would target another building and not mine. In wartime, man's humanity towards man is low on the survival scale.

Then there were those unbearable moments when buildings were blown to bits, bombed right out of existence; when bombs found buses, crowded with people. The next morning, after a heavy air raid, I'd walk past buildings that had been landmarks for all my life, now broken apart, smoldering shells of yesterday. After a while, though, I would no longer remember exactly what had been where, and I asked myself if this was to be my fate too—to become a mere shell of my many yesterdays, to be as quickly forgotten?

But fate had other plans. My new job, highly paid by British standards, was fairly dull (perhaps because of my total ignorance of anything scientific) but the scientists whom I worked among were far from dull, and I was soon to encounter a new world, one in which I would meet Art.

Bereavement and Beyond

It is not night when
I do see your face...

William Shakespeare

It's now eighteen months since Art has died, and while he continues to inhabit the depths of my house, that place where our souls meet, the upper stories still feel his absence. Existing within two overlapping levels, two distinct wavelengths, I float untethered between his reality and mine. While in his reality, I feel we are joined in communion and I'm back living a remembered sublimity. But within my own reality, that of the temporal with its day-to-day practicalities of taking care of the house, the garden, the finances, there are moments when I am overwhelmed with a recurring sense of desolation, the aloneness of a solo performer.

Before I was widowed, I facilitated bereavement groups and I remember pronouncing to the grieving members—with the comfortable conviction of the uninitiated—that our most abiding relationships never leave us, that we simply internalize them much as we internalize our parents. We hear their voices, see their faces, may even sense their hands in ours. They are impressions we cannot erase. Now, as I wander the house Art and I shared for forty years, the house in which we raised our children, I wonder if I could still make such a pronouncement.

My job, I tell myself, is to recognize the different wave-lengths within which I exist, knowing that while I'm in my practical mode, there is another deeper wavelength that I see with my inner eye. It is there, while meditating in the quiet of my room, that I meet my internalized "other" within an alliance fashioned beyond time. Endowed with a questing imagination, if I can free my mind from its usual constraints and enlarge my conditioned perception of but one reality, I am able to find that other realm. The realm in which Art is with me, touching my face with his hand, hugging me when I return from the store, holding me close as we fall asleep.

Each morning I step back and observe myself in my new life as a widow. I carry on with my usual exercise routine of dancing to Reggae or to Scott Joplin, oiling the bearings, loosening the joints. It is a routine that comforts me through stormy mornings, enabling me to move a threatening sadness to a lighter level. Times past, Art would remain in bed, watching me, relieved that he wasn't as compulsive as I. Some mornings I sense that Art is still in that bed watching me, and when I have finished dancing, we stay with each other for a while, connecting with intention across our two realities.

Recently, however, when the promise of another day failed to materialize in its usual way, I began to feel as if an unseen enemy was unraveling my slim defenses, a throwback to those early days after Art had died. I realized that I'd been thinking about him less often, had written him fewer letters. Sometimes an hour or two passed when I didn't think about him at all, didn't see his bearded face or hear his resonant voice. Later that morning, washing dishes, I looked out the window onto the garden Art had made and had a vision of him there in his old gardening slacks and even older white shirt. I realized then that my panic was about my fear of losing him, of letting him go. Were I to relax my passionate concentration on Art, might he slip out of my life and fade away like a forgotten photograph, blurred and lifeless, a darkened shadow of the original?

In my day-to-day existence, time imposes its own reality and I know that no matter how much I try to cling to Art, his image will ultimately blur and gradually diminish. Sometimes as I lunch with friends or attend a concert, my tears are forgotten for a magic moment, and I am hugged by my old happiness. But the curtain falls, the lights go on and then, driving home alone, I'm back clinging to this sad, empty space alongside me. Eventually, after hours, days, weeks, I remember what I've always known: my love for Art lives in my heart, unchanged, unchangeable.

I don't believe that bereavement is a straight path to a beckoning shore. Rather, it takes me on a capricious zig-zagging journey, one with Sisyphean overtones. And as I move along this unfamiliar rocky path, feeling more centered, time and again I find myself jerked back to my earliest grief: the grief I thought I had "dealt with." It happens whenever I find myself staring at an elderly couple holding hands, whenever I hear a certain piece of music or look at particular photographs. It happens when I touch Art's watch, his worn-out wallet, his keys—so much of him still around the house, waiting to capture my attention. Museum pieces from our youth together through our old age, his possessions conspire to catch me off guard and, for a while, I land right back on square one. At this point I have found the best thing—perhaps the only thing—to do is to shake hands with grief, as I would with an old respected friend, then turn around and walk right back to the present. I can never go back entirely to that which has left me, that which I have left.

I am thinking that there should be a Catechism According to the Bereaved, some gentle-bound truths to counter the many mistaken notions about bereavement, both for those living theirs and for those still apprehensive observers.

One of these notions is that after one year, we are presumed to be all mourned out. People, kind friends even, will imply that one is now ready to close the door on sorrow and resume a life unattended by grief and by tears. I am sure they mean well. It's just that they are entirely mistaken. It is true that time softens the initial blow, but I don't think I will ever completely seal up that door—and perhaps I shouldn't—for the act of mourning inspires my healing and incubates my sorrow, allowing for its gradual transformation.

Perhaps tears are a natural antidote to the anguish of an otherwise inexpressible grief. In the early days, I would not weep. But my body would soon shake from feeling my withholding and eventually break down. Occasionally there are still mornings when I wake up from a night's sleep with a deep sense of heaviness and restraint, and I know this feeling to be one of tears struggling to escape. One of my musings is that we humans are born with an endless reservoir of tears and joy—complementary twins—into which we dip or plunge, as the occasion arises, and that when I am with one, the other is not far away.

Another mistaken notion is that once a person has died, he or she has become an unmentionable, someone to be dropped from the roster, wiped off the slate and filed under Departed. To give voice to their name is to somehow commit an indelicate social blunder. Shortly after Art died, I was invited to a dinner party and decided to face this baptism by fire—my first time out alone. I hardly knew the other guests around the table, but they had known Art for many years as his colleagues. The evening passed slowly, the conversation distant from my interests, but I hoped to be an attentive guest. I was surprised, however, that no one mentioned Art's recent death or offered me a word of sympathy. After a while, I brought Art's name into the conversation, which resulted in an uneasy silence and a swift move made to another subject. Later, and somewhat belligerently, I again offered up Art's name, and again the same uneasy silence followed. I left early from that dinner and am sure the other guests must have been relieved. I don't fault them for what I assume to be their fears of mortality, but it made me realize how tender our culture is, how fearful of death so many of us are. And how needy we bereaved can be in the early months of our loss.

There are also those god-sent others: friends, acquaintances, even strangers who, by a miracle of innate empathy, manage to convey with a word—or even a touch—a compassion that warms my coldest parts. I am ever grateful when I am asked directly how I am doing. Facing someone's avoidance, only denigrates my sadness, as though all those yesterdays with Art had never happened.

Events tend to happen in clusters and death is no exception. Around the time of Art's death, many of my closest friends were also dealing with the loss of a partner; vigorous people suddenly faded and died. It felt as though some kind of hex had descended upon us all. In the mutuality of our grief, we sad ones rallied around each other and supported each other as we fled into the solace of feverish domesticity. One old friend remodeled her entire living area and another added a large studio onto her house. After Art's death, like a butterfly emerging from its chrysalis, I had several rooms in my house repainted in bright colors. It was an audacious act, tinged with guilt, as if I was celebrating a too early thaw, yet it yielded a momentary liberation from the darkness of grief.

In some ways, grieving the loss of Art has cut through my emotional complexities, opening me to the core so that, in all manner of things, I feel a new freedom. Shortly after Art died, a physicist friend of his visited from England. David and I share a deep friendship and he asked me if I had ever written about the feeling of being loved by loving? It's a question that has stuck in my mind. But the more I ponder, the less clear is my thinking—shades of the chicken and egg enigma cloud my thinking. Is my feeling of being loved by Art dependent on my first having loved him? Is it possible to love without the assurance of having been loved? It's a philosophical roundabout that confuses my mind.

Yet my heart seems to understand. I have an abiding sense of Art's love moving through my sorrow and comforting my soul. And alongside his love for me is my own expansive love for him, as we move in concert with one another across the illusion of separateness, embraced within a spiral of light, which has no beginning, no end. The world assumes a softer glow now—my corners having weathered into roundness; I've lost much of my former sharpness, and I don't think it has anything to do with the possible lassitude of old age. It has to do with love becoming visible.

Destination Unnamed

Death is the side of life
that is turned away from us . . .
There is neither a here nor a beyond
but the great unity.

Rainer Maria Rilke

This past year many of my close friends have died and I mourn their empty spaces. I feel like a broody mother hen trying to keep a family intact, only to find that some members are missing—taking part of me with them. At my age, the loss of a friend ruffles the serenity of my existence, and I am increasingly aware that death is a palpable presence, waiting in the wings to greet me as I too make my exit. How different from when I was young, when death was an event reserved for the unbelievably old, while I, in my innocence, lived under the illusion of immortality.

When I was ten, my mother took me to visit her ninety year-old grandmother who lay in a coma, close to death. My mother struggled—but failed—to express her grief, for there had been no love between the two women. In that austere, shaded bedroom, with its oversize dark oak Victorian wardrobe and two matching chests of drawers, standing in attendance like ladies-in-waiting, I carefully watched my great-grandmother. Intrigued and a little frightened, I listened to the sound of her embattled breathing. But I cannot remember feeling any sadness. She was a formidable personality to me; an unreachable icon, and I felt miserably inadequate in her presence. Once, when she was ill in bed, I spent days painstakingly writing her a letter in which I told her that, in my bedtime prayers, I was asking God to make her well. Eight years old at the time, it was written with the openhearted guilelessness of a child who had not yet learned the protective games of adulthood. My letter was promptly returned to me with every misspelled word heavily underlined. No encouraging words, nothing, only those black, accusatory marks. My great-grandmother's death was never mentioned in our house. As in so many other houses, death was a subject to be avoided. Even today, how often I hear the euphemism "passed away" for that word so hard for us to give voice to.

Years ago, as part of my hospice training, I had to write a short essay on my own death. I wrote quickly and from my head; today I would write it quite differently. For I see now that we die in concert with our own belief systems. If we strip death of its extraneous wrappings—our fear of pain; the loss, with all of its indignities, of our physical prowess; our farewells to all those people and things we so love—what is left? I think that what remains is the strength of our own persuasions, those beliefs we have formed, religious or secular, during our lives. These are our companions, the luggage we take with us on our journey.

I became a hospice volunteer in 1982 and during the next ten years witnessed many such journeys. My work within the hospice community remains an unforgettable, even a holy experience, as I observed patients move from the known to an unknown. And with few exceptions, despite all the rigors and sadness of leaving, I sensed that their vision was clear and their road maps intact.

The day I met Andy, my first patient, I rang the doorbell to his home and, in spite of the intensive training I had been given and the fact that I considered myself a seasoned counselor, I had a bad case of nerves. Standing on that porch, everything I had learned vanished from my mind and panic moved in. I felt like an unprepared angel of death. I found the family inside assembled in the living room, ready to greet me. It was a tender moment as we looked at each other. Could the grieving family trust me with their sorrow? And what could I give to them of my heart? When we moved into the bedroom and I saw Andy, I said, "Hello, I'm Joan." And he said, "Hello Kate," which was his wife's name. The family corrected him but he would have none of it. So I said, "Call me Kate if you wish, it's one of my favorite names." He studied me for an unsettling moment and then he burst out laughing, and that was when we met.

An artist, Andy painted on huge canvases that covered the walls of the barn-like house he had built. He was a man who had pursued his dreams, some of which he realized, though many he was never to own. In his early twenties with a friend, he bought a single engine plane and started an airline, flying cargo overnight. Before the airline failed, he owned six planes and employed sixty people. A restless, driven man, not without rage, he was as unforgiving of his own failings as he was intolerant of the frailties of others. Black-bearded like an indomitable Moses, he would have scared me had I known him earlier. Now, however, he was immobilized, dying from a brain tumor and bereft of everything that had once defined him. One afternoon, a few weeks after we met, his eyes speaking what his voice could not, he motioned for me to read from a book about South Africa, the country of his childhood. As I read, he wept from the deepest parts of his soul. We were to repeat this pattern on many occasions—my reading, his weeping—but each time he wept, he appeared to be escaping from a jail into sunlight.

As Andy got closer to death, his earlier strivings became muted and transformed into a kind of serenity such as I doubt he had never known. It was as if something within, some endorphin-like quality, was smoothing his journey. A unique bonding occurred at this stage between us: two people, one so near to leaving and the other staying around for a while longer. And because death has no time for social amenities, the trust and intimacy that otherwise would have taken years to obtain, was reached between us almost immediately. Perhaps the knowledge that we are all dying brings with it a freedom to be ourselves, to be totally vulnerable with one another, much as a newborn bonds instinctively with its mother. Andy died listening to his favorite Bach record with his wife, Kate, and his family with him. He was forty-four years old.

Caroline, another patient, lived a different story. When I rang her doorbell early one spring morning, an unexpectedly vigorous voice ordered me to *Come in!* Caroline was propped up in bed in a room that looked like an executive's work station: two telephones, yellow legal pads and newspapers were scattered around her, and a large television screen faced her bed. In one corner sat her oxygen tank. On her bedside table, an ashtray held a pack of cigarettes. We greeted each other and she instructed me to put my coat on a chair, then, hardly pausing to take a breath, she ordered me to straighten up her bedside table, tidy the bedroom, and be sure to heat up the supper that her household help had prepared. One false move on my part, and she would loudly proclaim *No, not there, it belongs over here!* Suffering from lung cancer, Caroline, was an angry, embittered soul, and she was dying the way she had lived, by defying any semblance of vulnerability. Her son and daughter, who lived nearby, appeared from time to time, though with obvious reluctance. One afternoon as I was busily scuttling around, she burst out with *How I love to order you around!* And I replied, *You certainly do!* We looked at each other, neither of us saying a word, and I was astonished by the expression on her face, which habitually was one of watchful rigidity. Now, however, she was smiling with the sly glee of a malevolent Cheshire cat— a cat that knows how to manipulate its world— and I melted into an uncontrolled giggle. It was our first intimate moment and the beginning of our friendship.

Each time I visited, Caroline would recount the daily drama: her doctor who had failed to return her many telephone calls; her feckless household help whom she suspected of unloading her refrigerator; her friends who irritated her. Her world was one of dissonance and distrust. Life was slipping away from her and she resolutely summoned all of her survival strategies. It worked for a while and she moved out of hospice care. Three months later she died, on her terms. In an ironic way, she was in control until the end.

* * *

In Western culture, life and death are often presented as adversaries, combatants in a duel for time. We have been conditioned to think of death as an ending, as something to be feared. But life is by nature a chain of beginnings and endings. No sooner are we secure in one phase than we are propelled— sometimes with great reluctance— into the next, where we must again face the challenges of the unknown. The pause between an ending and a new beginning may be experienced as loss, but aren't death and resurrection woven into the pattern of our existence as endlessly as day follows night?

As the territory between my life and my death shrinks, there are moments when I feel an affinity with something *out there,* some *other.* It's as if life and death are comrades, evolving towards something that, at an intuitive level, feels like the next step on a journey whose itinerary is incomplete and whose destination is unnamed. I ask myself if this is perhaps how I felt earlier within the aquatic confines of the womb—where, I've read, we already have some vision and ability to hear our world. It is tempting to believe that we continue this pattern: a flowing outward into an environment waiting to receive us.

Solitude

The world is too much with us; late and soon...

William Wordsworth

My neighbor's cat lives in my garden. She is aware of me, aware of herself. These days we maintain an agreed distance. A truce. Ten years ago, the cat and Art would converse in a mutuality of purring cat language, while I, in my fury at finding mangled birds, would storm outside, berate Art and send that infidel firmly on her way. The loss of Art, however, has gentled my nature and softened my impatience over things I cannot control. Nowadays I leave cat and bird to shape their own destinies.

Black as a mahogany Madonna, the cat rests on the fecund soil among the scarlet-flowered salvia bushes, a few feet away from the bird feeder. She invites no one. Should a neighborhood cat offer companionship, it is swiftly repulsed. From my window I admire—with a trace of envy—the independence and the undeviating sense of purpose of my uninvited guest as she settles into her instinctive nature. Motionless for hours, she has found her place of a defined aloneness.

I continue to battle for mine as I confront the unrelenting pull of conflicting desires: those that yearn for the comfort of friends, and those that ache to be alone in the silence of my room. Only in the silence do my thoughts and I hear each other, as the unquiet world outside rocks to its cacophonous beat, energizing the young and exhausting the elderly. There is, though, an excitement for the elderly in that beat, since it propels us to focus on the present rather than nesting in the past. At lunch yesterday at a restaurant, I was unable to hear my companion through the buzz of voices and the unceasing din of cutlery against plates. She suggested that I de-activate one of my digital hearing aids, and I was, once again, grateful for modern technology.

Such gratitude, however, is tempered by opposing thoughts as I catch myself whining about the prevailing addiction to cell phones, iPods and blaring car stereos—items without which their owners remain confined to the rigors of silence. Shopping on Fourth Street in Berkeley some years ago, I rested on a bench outside a cafe where a middle-aged man was relaxing in the sun. We exchanged neighborly smiles and I delved into my purse for my list. "It's a perfect day," he said. Pursuing my list, I answered with an enthusiastic "Gorgeous." Then I heard, "How about meeting for lunch?" My thoughts zipped from my shopping list to a more pleasing venture and, with my most gracious smile, I turned around to answer. By now, my neighbor had walked a few feet away from the bench and appeared to be looking off into the distance, talking to the air: it took a few seconds before I realized that I'd been upstaged by a cell phone.

Nowadays, the cell phone is a permanent attachment to our anatomy. A facilitator of our fractured lives, it is also the enabler of unending verbal dramas, often accompanied by expressions of frozen anxiety. We are thus exposed to the sometime intimate lives of our neighbors—an embarrassment for me, since in my youth it was considered a mortal sin to eavesdrop.

To some degree I empathize with the present generation of noisemakers, since in England, in the twenties and thirties, I was up there among the noisiest. But our noise was different. In those days, telephones operated with the assistance of overworked operators who plugged you into your connection, which emitted more static than audibility. Radios tended to splutter and crackle for only a few hours each day, broadcasting a single station. Coveted by the masses, they were mostly owned by the moneyed classes. Television didn't arrive until the 1940's. And if an airplane appeared, we would watch, with awe and disbelief, this mysterious object with wings, floating high in the sky with it's ominous rumble. That was our noise. On a more personal level, I'd dance at our local Palais-de-Dance where the band drove its rhythm right through the roof, dine at jam-packed, intimate cafes in Soho and drink illegal drinks at clamorous nightclubs, following the noise whenever invited. Then, I could take it or leave it. Now, there is no leaving.

Toward the end of World War II, Art and I left an embattled London for the United States. We arrived in Manhattan where I was captivated by the skyscrapers reaching heavenward, the endless abundance of exotic foods and the warmth of its inhabitants. The following year we moved to Massachusetts, where I caught my first glimpse of quietude.

Early one November morning Art and I walked around Walden Pond in Concord. We were totally alone in that pristine, hushed place, heavy with the pending silence of winter. Holding onto Art's hand, I became the traveler whose head received information but whose heart felt a fear in that unaccustomed solitude. For me, aloneness translated into lonely, lonely into abandonment, and abandonment into unknown dangers. The next day I wandered into a bookstore in Cambridge, bought *Walden* and read every word of Thoreau's account of his life in the woods. It was then I began to listen to myself.

I was blessed with a mother-in-law who loved me, despite our being opposites in personalities. Alice was a self-effacing woman of quiet obstinacy, who trod gently and expressed few contrary opinions. Art and I were often troubled by her seeming passivity. When the children were young, Alice would visit us regularly. Upstairs on the couch in our living room, she'd observe our daily drama, sitting for hours in silent contemplation with a book of poems resting on her lap. She frequently quoted her favorite line from Browning: "The best is yet to be," which I interpreted as a certain helpless renunciation of the moment. I was critical then of what appeared to be her premature drifting into a self-imposed exile—into a state of nothingness.

Sixty years later, less judgmental and hopefully a little wiser, I watch as I, too, withdraw from the events of the day, and I understand now that this moving inward is not a retreat into a meaningless void; rather it is a shift of energy into self. In my youth, time was a given—born with the universe, unending. But, as my own pace slows, that of time—the arbiter of existence—speeds up like a whirlwind, and snatches away yet another one of my priceless days.

In my old age, I sense an emerging farewell. The music softens, the dance slows, and the road—no longer forward seeking—circles back to its beginnings and beckons primordial images. I am dressed in a blue pleated tunic, sitting at a wooden desk on the first day of kindergarten. Holding a piece of chalk in my hesitant fingers, I struggle to form the letters of my name, as Miss Austin—surely the role model for Dickens bleakest teachers—stands alongside, ruler in hand, all too ready to rap my knuckles in disapproval. A small day school, run by two maiden ladies, I smell the paraffin oil stove in the corner of the room, alongside which errant pupils sit facing the bare wall. I am back with the 'who' of me, the self I left behind, as I maneuvered my irresolute way through the seasons of my years. I think of how, through the twistings and turnings of existence, and the grit and grime of survival, the ultimate prize is this reconciliation with the original unvarnished self.

These days, I increasingly turn down invitations from close friends and worry that I'm shutting up shop too soon, that it's dark inside with no lights. It is a tricky balance, dependent upon both energy and intent. The need to be with my aloneness demands a solitude to which I willingly return. I am mindful of my friend Seth who used to invite me for tea: a voluble, charming host. He'd make the tea, and I'd take the cookies he offered. As he grew older, though, after about an hour together, sometimes less, he'd softly suggest that perhaps I'd better leave, since he was concerned about my driving through heavy traffic. I now understand this as his way of reclaiming his solitude.

Moving into self is not always a gentle voyage. Alone for a few days, immersed in writing or just being, there are times when without warning my comfort begins to unravel; fear insinuates and I am momentarily trapped in the aching loneliness of a sojourner on a silent, icy planet. It is the price the trickster-gods, in their hubris, extract from us humans who dare to choose. Sometimes I panic. Sometimes I simply wait for the spell to pass. But eventually the emergent sun melts the ice, and I am back home, hugging a solitude of my own design.

The Crucible of Christmas

Happiness is beneficial for the body
but it is grief that develops the powers of the mind.

Marcel Proust

"Keep your porch light on," the dispatcher at 911 instructed. I said I would. Early December, rainy and cold, I got out of bed, dressed in my new black turtleneck and made up my face. The pain in my chest was more pronounced now and my shuddering heart was revving up its engines, as if to prepare for imminent take-off. I walked upstairs, switched on the outside light, sat at the dining room table—and waited.

* * *

At Alta Bates Hospital, an earnest, young cardiologist sat by my bedside and explained that I had pericarditis, an inflammatory infection, probably caused by a virus that simulates a heart attack. By then, my heart was pumping happily and had simmered down to a steady, untroubled beat. He advised me that I could go home, but then carefully asked if I had given any thought to my end-of-life decisions, a question that startled me, since an imminent ending was not on my mind; my thoughts having more to do with the imminent arrival of my family, my unwritten holiday cards and my anxiety-ridden joy of matching favorite gifts to favorite people. But I do recollect checking the beat of my heart more cautiously in the days following, half-expecting it to complete its aborted take-off. My continuing unease, however, had less to do with my physical well-being than with my fluctuating emotions, since at this time of the year it is my mind that is the trouble-maker.

Thanksgiving held no hostages but the crucible of Christmas was too soon upon me. It was time now to fill in the sharp, wounding edges, smooth out the surface, and rewrite the story with its cast of characters, long cloistered in the guarded recesses of memory. This year Christmas would be different, I told myself. But my intractable mind had other ideas and I drifted back into the domain of my English childhood.

* * *

We had our tree with Christmas candles and rubicund Santas in attendance, along with silver stars and red, green and gold metallic balls, back from their year-long hibernation in the basement. The tree stood in our dining room, by the balcony, which looked onto the street where no matter the weather—raging winds, to pelting rain, to the occasional glimmer of winter sun—groups of carolers congregated in the streets, warmed by their passion for the season. On hearing the strains of "Joy to the World" or "Good King Wenceslas," Doreen and I raced from the balcony down to the street and handed out chocolates and sometimes pennies for a good cause. Christmas was a heady, anticipatory time, of children's parties (routinely followed by a dose of castor oil to counter impure eating) and later, of parties with school friends, and later still, of maneuverings under well-placed mistletoe for that expectant kiss.

For my father, it was the busiest time of the year; he'd leave our home for his butcher shop at around four a.m. and return close to midnight. We saw less of him than usual and, as always, I watched every anguished move of my mother as she played her role with a brittle, restless gaiety, weary to her bones, unrelentingly consumed with anger and resentment toward my father for his infidelities. For her, Christmas was another performance, a secular affair, to be endured.

Then there were those other houses: the houses of my grandparents. The houses we visited at Christmas-time.

My father's mother and stepfather owned a brick-and-timbered house in Oxshott, a well-bred village in the county of Surrey, southwest of London. Surrounded by vast lawns, a conservatory and a tennis court, to the uninitiated eye the house embodied the grace and well being of its presumed class. Inside, though, a less benign script played out. A heavy front door opened onto an entrance hall furnished with a grandfather clock, high backed chairs, oak bookcases, and rugs designed to pleasure the discerning eye. To the right, a winding staircase led up to the bedrooms and above that the upper-most floors held the attic rooms for the household staff. Arriving Christmas morning by train, the familiar charade soon began. My mother and my grandmother, united only in their shared loathing, circled around each other with contrived amicability—two women in the heat of the feminine, awaiting the exact moment to pounce. My sister and I were instructed to take off our shoes in order to not offend the rugs, while my father, the indulged son, glided through the tempest with his usual aplomb. My step-grandfather, a gentle, detached being, greeted us kindly and thereafter reappeared mostly at mealtimes. It was a house that did not know the warmth of hugs; a house that shuddered at the impact of children. For my mother it was an unmitigated disaster of her own design.

Given to instant pronouncements, particularly in matters of refinement, my mother had early on labeled her mother-in-law a common uneducated cockney who lacked even the lower middle-class social amenities. Over the years, my mother, who blamed her own failing marriage on the fact that she had married ' beneath her,' would publicly correct my grandmother's prose (as she did my father's) and then icily enunciate the errant word, in the manner of an elocution teacher addressing a class of benighted students. For me, as a child, it was all part of the play we lived, and nobody dared interrupt the narrative.

My mother did not sleep during the three or four days we stayed in that house. Each night, consumed by premonitions of disaster, she sat on a chair by the bedroom window and gazed into the garden, joined only by the cold comfort of pale moonlight, as she waited for dawn to break. And each morning she appeared at breakfast, her usual vivacious self, dressed in one of her flamboyant creations, yielding not one whit to her adversary. It was, my mother told me later, a house of evil intent.

On Christmas morning, Doreen and I sat in our expected silence, intimidated by the conversation that in no way included us. The adults were served the requisite first course of half a grapefruit, an expensive item in those times, while we children faced a timid half of an orange. My grandfather, in his quiet manner, enquired of my grandmother why the children had only half of an orange. The conversation stopped abruptly, my grandmother attempted a flustered explanation, but she knew her limits with my grandfather. The bell was pressed, the maid appeared, and my sister and I, paralyzed with the unaccustomed attention and fearful of our grandmother's wrath, received our grapefruit. To the outward eye, the benevolent angel of Christmas hovered around that house, but to the inner eye of the child it was a place haunted by fallen angels.

After my parents separated when I was twelve, I never visited that house again. My mother, my sister and I were swiftly excommunicated, erased from the family, and like yesterday's sandcastles, swept away by an implacable sea.

* * *

My mother's father and his second wife lived in East Molesey, also in the county of Surrey and close by Hampton Court Palace, home to King Henry VIII. Their house sat on the outskirts of town and emerged at the end of a long driveway, shrouded by dense hedges. During WW II, while job hunting in London, I stayed there for a couple of weeks, and the dark, solitary walk from the gates to a view of the house always caused me to shiver, as if danger awaited. Three stories, with decorative eaves and a turreted roof, it stood in the midst of lawns presided over by a life-size eighteenth century marble statue of a comely young woman—a trophy from my grandparent's travels in Europe. At the far end of the garden, the Mole River, a tributary of the Thames, meandered by and, on occasion, a punt or row boat drifted into view. The sprawling grounds, with a dilapidated summerhouse tucked among the encircling trees, offered a haven for children to roam and to climb—and to hide.

My grandparents welcomed us warmly enough into their home, but it was not a tender place where a child could be assured of a touch or a hug or a simple comfort that consoles. Or even of the intimacy of familial disagreement. There was an implied Keep Out cautionary zone of watchfulness between parents and children; a shadowy, unsafe bridge that no one attempted to cross.

At Christmas the main house came alive, decorated with holly and mistletoe, paper chains looped over the banisters, and a giant Christmas tree in the dining room with offerings spread around the floor. At dinner, the children sat at a side table with their paper hats and firecrackers while the adults gathered around the refectory table. Glancing at my mother, I'd see the tight smile she used in this house and was aware there was no joy here, that nobody really liked anyone. The conversations felt punctuated with uneasy starts that lingered, like forlorn orphans, in the disjoint of the unspoken.

My grandfather parented seven children, three with his first wife who died at the age of twenty-one—my mother was their oldest child—and four with Alice, his second wife, whom I called Aunt Alice, and whose children I thought of as cousins since we were all close in age. After the sudden death of his first wife, my grandfather took to drinking and it was Alice, the auburn-haired barmaid at the local pub, who made sure he arrived home safely.

He set Alice up in a flat where three of their four children were born. They finally married just before the birth of Irene, their youngest child. For the rest of his life my grandfather would have periods of heavy drinking, and it was to Alice he always turned. She never failed him.

Recently, I unearthed a photo of the family in the garden dated 1926: my Grandfather and Aunt Alice sit in wicker chairs, my parents stand stiffly apart, separated by my mother's sister, Dolly, and her family. The six of us children, Irene, myself, Frank, Doreen, Gwen, and Joe, ranging in age from seven to sixteen, sprawl on the grass as Buller, the English bull dog, whose face is ferocious but whose heart is golden, keeps guard. I place the photo back on my desk, and then pick it up again, as if its fragility needs some kind of comfort. I study it more carefully with a magnifying glass, feeling an inexpressible sadness for those children on the grass. But I quickly push my sadness away as I want to stay with memories of Christmas, when we played hide-and-seek and murder all through the house and into its dark cellars; when we rowed on the River Mole and trudged to Hampton Court Palace....where one long, cold afternoon I got lost in its maze, and when, in my mid-teens, Frank and I escaped to the local dance hall and flirted in our shy, fumbling way. But like ghosts tapping at my window, the past weaves into the present and the sadness returns, and I weep for Joe, dying in the early months of the war as his plane went down over Malta; for Irene who, after an unrelenting manic-depression, committed suicide in her mid-forties, and for Gwen, in and out of mental institutions for over twenty years and who would write me later that both she and Irene had, as children, been molested by their father—my grandfather.

* * *

"How was your Christmas?" my friend Karen asks a few days into the New Year. And I reply —the way I always do—"it was

110

just lovely." But was it lovely? I've continued to celebrate Christmas here in the house where Art and I lived for over forty years, as it provides a bulwark against the chasm of his absence. But Art's leaving unlocked more truths than I cared to face, and this year I realized that I was still—at ninety—that child watching the grown-ups around the table caught in their theater of deception. Only now the grown-ups are me and my own family: my children, Jonathan and Jennifer, my grandchildren, Adam and Megan—and through marriages and divorces and remarriages, all the people who are now part of my new family who come together each year to celebrate.

This year, as in past years, I braced for the inevitable obstacle race I knew I could not win. Had Art been here with me, despite his agnosticism and his aversion to ceremony, he would have brought his good humor to my strivings to mandate the perfect event—the way it's supposed to be. He'd play his favorite Gilbert and Sullivan song on his accordion, and later, we'd rally around the piano, the children playing their flutes and recorders. For a moment there, I might have slipped out of my vigilance and felt safe. Happy even. Our daughter, Jennifer, who brings joy along with her, would have loved it; our son, Jonathan, newly remarried, so like his father in his resistance to ceremony, would be eager to introduce his new wife to Art, and Art, in his love for me would have endured—perhaps even secretly enjoyed it all—while I, exhausted and diminished, sighed with relief when the decorations were once again tucked away in the basement.

But Art is not here with me, and the obstacle race is still around. This year, sitting in the living room, listening to the family chat, I caught myself wishing that instead of exchanging breezy quips to soften uneasy spaces, we would speak directly to each other. I fantasized about the joys of a family love-in reminiscent of the ageless flower children of the sixties, in their search for the authentic. It was then I realized that my role has always been to soothe our gatherings, and not incidentally my own comfort zone, by coaxing the family into an affability of emptiness where everything is said about nothing. That I, too, have played my own disingenuous games of avoidance by being the anxious observer—rarely the joyful participant—in our family Christmases. This year, more than anything, I have learned that family portraits not only exhibit the devout respectability of a Norman Rockwell painting, but they also project the landscape of our fears, our discontents, even our yearnings. I have learned, too, that we may choose to paint over primal images, to hold close the present and to envision that which is possible with our more seasoned, more nuanced eye: the eye that lives in the cradle of all of our hearts.

Circle of Dispossession

In order to possess what you do not possess
You must go by the way of dispossession.

T.S. Eliot

Packing to go on a journey, no matter how alluring, evokes near hysteria in me. I make long lists and agonize, filling every inch of my largest suitcase. Inevitably, though, I end up using the same few items, like my well-worn black pants, my saggy wool sweater and my zip-up all-weather loafers; comfort clothing—signposts directing me back to me. Without my soul baggage I am a fugitive in enemy territory.

At my audiologist's office in downtown Oakland last Friday, an elderly man danced into the waiting room. Thin and tiny, he looked at me, said something in a strange tongue, and then broke into little gusts of giggles. Dressed in eye-catching new clothes that hung almost apologetically on his slight frame, he sat on the chair opposite me and gestured as if he wanted to write, so I handed him a pen. Very slowly, on a small piece of paper, he drew the letters of his name, carefully pronouncing each letter in English. But his name made no sense to me. I asked him if he came from China, and after a long response, I gathered that he came from an island near Vietnam. Pointing to a closed door decorated with the familiar skirt and pants, he continued to talk and laugh, prodding the door nervously with his umbrella. I

113

wasn't sure how to tell him to proceed down the hall to another doctor's office, knock at the glass window, and ask for the key to the toilet. The confusion ended, however, when a secretary appeared with the key, and the man's nervousness changed into unmistakable relief along with what I assumed were his ecstatic thank yous.

As I sat waiting for my name to be called, I felt an inexplicable tenderness toward this stranger, whose eyes saw mostly incomprehensible signs but whose body danced the language of connection. I wondered about the country he had left behind—the last time he had walked upon his native soil and touched his familiar loves. Did he leave by choice, or was his leaving an imposed renunciation of everything he had ever been?

The last time is on my mind these days. My eyesight less sharp, I no longer drive across the Bay Bridge into San Francisco at night. No longer do I drive in combative traffic to the Marin Headlands to roam its wild beaches, and no longer do I pick up friends at the airport, since my energy too soon collapses like a dejected soufflé. At ninety, the last time bids its whispered farewell—which my ears do not want to hear—as it nudges me gently off the tracks and onto the sidelines of memory. I try to recollect the exact moment my body withdrew into its quieter mode, so that I might hug it in gratitude for its past fidelity. But I cannot, since my short-term memory has become hazy. Today, after working in the garden among the roses and the unbowed gladiolus, I rested there awhile as I searched my mind—and failed—to recollect the name of a tree I'd planted about five years ago. A fragile beauty then, it now towers alongside the bamboo offering its masses of purple blossoms. Faced with a slackening memory, my reaction is always the same: first I fuss, then I demand and, ultimately, I beseech. My mind is a blank page. It is only in the empty silence that I discover I need to take a deep breath, to let go of demands and, with reverential simplicity, hand the problem over to my inner self, the guardian of my well being. Then, at unexpected moments, the answer rises into awareness like the morning sun. Ah, it's a Mexican Mallow!

Long-term memory, though, is more willing to cooperate

and offers up nostalgic glimpses of my frivolous eighties, when I dashed hither and yon, up and down the steps to my house, in and out of my car. I would cavort with friends and end the day, admittedly, a trifle fatigued, but never flat-out exhausted—a condition I consigned to the provenance of the ancients. But now, I am one of them. My memory frequently wanders off on its own mission, seemingly unattached to me, as it reflectively trolls to earlier beginnings, to kaleidoscopic images of first-times, that primogenitor of last-times. And I wonder if this is some kind of gentle compensation for fading neurons, or if there is a more compelling need that is pushing for recognition? Since I have steadfast faith in the veracity of my somewhat contentious mind, I am forced to accept that it is unveiling a message that is not diversionary but is rather god-sent.

* * *

Ten years old, in my first year of secondary school, I am the youngest in a class of twenty-five students. I am also the class clown who, between periods, entertains to great acclaim, mimicking the teachers and performing handstands. Since my unflinching aim is to retain the love and admiration of my peers, I willingly pay the price of being caught and sent to the head mistress who terrifies my dreams. The bell rings, I scamper to my desk, our room teacher, Mrs. Duffield, arrives. Standing in respectful silence we chant our *good mornings* and are instructed to be seated. And then, I fart. It is the kind of fart that resonates with the intensity of a thunderbolt. The student in front of me swings around as if struck by lightening and yells into my face: *Joan Hill!* I am the center of attention, the place for which I yearn, but now, my face flushed crimson, I wish to die.

A digression: In England of the 1920's, it was a sine qua non that members of the lower classes who lusted after upward migration, engage in behavior consummate with the social graces of their betters. And, in true British call-to-arms, they became adept at assuming a false gentility. Among countless transgressions, one's bodily functions were crude unmentionables, to be repressed at all cost: to audibly fart was tantamount to a blasphemy beyond redemption. Faced with an uncontrollable dilemma, one clenched one's teeth and prayed.

* * *

It's summer. My mother, Doreen, and I travel from London by train, to an East Coast seaside town. Our daily routine is to walk down to the beach, carrying our buckets and spades, and to search for a patch of soft sand among the rocks and pebbles that hug the coastline. The water is freezing and, together with a small group of children from the boarding house, I wait around in my swim suit, my extremities turning purple and my teeth chattering, partly from the cold but mostly in abject terror, since it is soon my turn to be thrown into the sea. This is the way we are taught to swim. One of the guests in our boarding house is a captain in the British Army. He brings his young son to the beach, and we are all captivated by the captain's impressive uniform and his fearless dives into the rough water. Noticing our collective fears, he suggests to the parents that he give us daily lessons. He is especially patient with me, since I am the most timid. He takes my hand and walks me into the water, gently coaxing me away from my fear of being thrown in and lost forever, to a place where I begin to feel relatively secure. He insists on giving me extra lessons, and I bask in his attention. The captain becomes my special seaside-friend. Back at the house, he plays with me after lunch, hoisting me onto his shoulders and takes me for rides up to the top floor. I am five years old. I am the chosen one.

One afternoon, up there on his shoulders, I feel something move inside my panties. Then it stops moving and I quickly decide that it is nothing, only my imagination. The following afternoon the same thing happens. This time, though, it is a probing hand. I feel a shocking fear that something is not right, that I shouldn't be there,

116

that something bad is happening. The next day is a repetition of the day before, but this time the hand is more insistent, and I wriggle down off the captain's shoulders and tell him that I have to go. In a curious way, I am both frightened and exhilarated. I tell nobody about these episodes, certainly not my mother. It is my private secret.

The next afternoon, my sister and I decide to play a game of cards in our bedroom. Our room is next to the bathroom, at the end of a dark passageway. As we get close to the bathroom, the door opens to reveal a man, standing there, totally naked, with something black and furry and huge standing up from out of him. The man beckons us, saying: " Look, come touch." I stand there, paralyzed, momentarily forgetting my own identity, as if his command is final. The grimacing face of the man is vaguely familiar, but the expression in his eyes is nothing I have seen before; it is that of a vicious, panting animal about to pounce. And then I recognize my special friend, the captain. Breaking the spell, my sister grabs my hand and we escape into our bedroom. We move the heavy chest of drawers against the door and then the table, and then anything else that will move, and await the struggle. There is no way to call for help other than beyond our barricade and, for hours, we remain glued against the furniture. Around dinnertime, we creep out into the deserted passageway and go to find our mother.

* * *

Seventeen years old, I am vacationing in Lugano, Switzerland with my mother. Alone one Monday morning, I walk into town to browse its local street market. Stalls line the square, offering cheeses, chocolates, miniature hand-painted music boxes and wooden clocks. At one stall, I chat with an elderly man who is playing a soulful accordion serenade to his family of toys. It seems not to matter that neither of us know the other's language, and we end up smiling our happy good-byes, like old friends who share a secret past. The scene reminds me of an English country fair that has forsaken its inhibitions and is indulging in a bacchanalian exuberance of spirit. I wander among the crowds awhile, making notes of needed translations, and then relax on a nearby bench to check my ever-present dictionary. Moments later, a gentle touch on my arm finds me gazing into a sleeked black-haired twin to Rudolph Valentino. In a mix of Italian, French, and English he asks if he might be of help. He tells me his name is Marco, and his sympathetic eyes and intriguing accent melt my usual shyness.

Back in the market, we spend the next hour together, he the tutor and I the student. He tells me that he is a Swiss guide, employed by Thomas Cooks' Travel Agency—incidentally, the agency in London through whom we've booked our trip—and that he is happy, honored even, to help me repair my French. Perhaps we can meet for coffee tomorrow? I am flattered, and indeed grateful, that this urbane, thirty-two year old Swiss wishes to spend time with me. During that week we meet a couple more times and take amiable walks along the shore of Lake Lugano. My French is visibly improving and I feel I have found a new friend. Marco is to guide a group to Milan, Italy the following week, and he wonders whether, before he leaves, he might take me to his favorite bar about twenty-five kilometers out of town. The bar is owned by his friend Nino and is a place where, he assures me, I will meet the locals, since tourists rarely venture that far. On Saturday, driving in his car along the lake and up into the hills, and buoyed by the warm wind and the sunshine, I sense the sweet enticement of romance, but quickly counter such wishful thinking with a reminder that Marco's interest is decidedly more brotherly than amorous.

Bar Nino is already crowded when we arrive. Live music is playing and couples dance on an improvised floor, others sit at tables, drinking and throwing dice. Decorated with corncobs and salami stringed to colored lights projecting from the ceiling, the place holds a vaguely dissolute air that unexpectedly jars me, as if there is only a brooding darkness here; a darkness where wearied souls might escape into yet another night of forgetfulness. It is not the bucolic scene of my eager imagination. Nino comes over to greet us and takes us to a reserved table, away from the beat of the music and near a flight of stairs that lead to rooms above. Friends of Marco's drop by to chat and since the conversation is entirely in Switzadeutsch, a German dialect I cannot understand, I sit there, silent and lonely, and more than a little piqued at Marco who, contrary to his usual attentiveness, seems to be ignoring me. Meanwhile, the waiter arrives with a flagon of red wine, and I lose no time in taking a few welcome sips. Then, quickly, the room begins to spin around and everything dissolves into a faceless blur. Unable to focus, and feeling an unexpected drowsiness, I stand, but my legs are unable to obey my head. M body, seemingly directionless, begins its slide into the oblivion of sleep. For a moment I panic and will my eyes to please stay open. But it is a losing battle. . . .

Midway up the stairs, the last thing I remember is gazing down into the haze of smoke and people, and thinking that there has to be one person down there who knows me, one person who cares. But nobody hears my thoughts. And the hand that holds firmly to mine, leads us on and up.

The pain between my legs breaks my sleep, and through a blurred consciousness, I become aware of someone beside me on a bed, and of some thing probing and pushing hard up into me. Limp, like a discarded rag doll, and unable yet to talk, I recognize Marco; a furious, deranged, yelling Marco. And I know that it is his hand there. I don't think I feel fear, or, in fact, anything, other than a resigned passivity. After a while, Marco, faced with the challenge of an impenetrable virgin changes his plans; his yelling subsides. He moves away from the bed. He sits on a chair, and stares a cold hatred into me. I dress and, without a word, follow him down those stairs, through the empty bar and out into the night. Stone-faced and in total silence, he drives me back to my hotel.

At breakfast the next morning, my mother asks if I enjoyed the evening with my new friend. I tell her that I had. I lock the incident away, deep in my mind, telling no one. Until now.

* * *

119

April, 1949, I am five months pregnant with my second child. Our son, Jonathan, is three. Art is teaching at MIT and plans to take the summer off to build our new house in nearby Lexington; meanwhile, I am the support system, delegated to keep the enterprise running smoothly. Normally I'm a happy manager, but fate intervenes, and after two days with a blinding headache, I am hospitalized with the diagnosis of polio. It turns out to be a light case and I am back, somewhat shakily, on my feet just in time to give birth.

Since I am full-term, and increasingly fearful that the polio might have harmed my baby, my obstetrician decides to induce labor. (He also, it turns out, has a vacation planned.) A genial, Boston Brahman type, highly commended among our friends, it is his habit to ease his patients into a deep sleep at the first signs of dilation. I have no problem with this.

In the hospital, as I drift into sleep, I am aware of being moved onto a gurney and of people hovering around, and then of the pressure of something pushing up inside of my belly, up and into the aqueous paradise of my unborn. But above all, I am aware of an enveloping rage, unlike any I have experienced—a rage that obliterates everything but itself. Hours later, I awake to a moment of ineffable joy: I am holding my daughter, Jennifer, a dark-eyed, bald-headed bundle.

At my six-week checkup, I sit opposite Dr. Harley-Smith in his well-tempered office. After the usual post-delivery instructions, we chat awhile on less formal matters. A handsome man in his late sixties, and an ardent anglophile, which in Boston is not a disadvantage, we have fallen into an easy doctor/patient relationship. I ask him about his vacation and he asks me about our new house. Then he swings his armchair around and, looking directly into my eyes, he asks if I remember anything that I said during the delivery. I assure him I do not. He then asks if I want to know what I said. I stare at him and see a challenge in his eyes—or is it a threat?— that mystifies and scares me. To back down, however, will imply a certain "wimpishness" of character,

120

so I smile brightly and tell him to go right ahead.

"The words you used, in no uncertain terms, were: *get your fucking hands out of me,*" he says.

"Absolutely not," I counter. "I've never, ever, used that word. To have uttered that word would have burned the skin off my lips."

"But you said it."

"I did not,"

"Indeed you did," he responds.

Ultimately, I give in and wonder what evoked so deep a profanity.

* * *

Today, I reflect on the road back though time, and I am a bit shaken. These are not the endearing, god-sent messages I have envisioned; they are, rather, reminders of inexpressible angst from a past that I'd as soon keep veiled in perpetual obscurity. Smarting from what I feel is a distinct lack of empathy, I decide to ignore my mind. But the messenger persists: "You asked didn't you? Look again." I look hard, once more, down through the lens of memory, through layer upon layer of obscuration, until I recognize the reservoirs of disillusion and fear—and, specifically, of shame. They are all waiting there, disconsolate, like unclaimed baggage. I am filled with a tenderness, and an urge to melt the amnesia of yesteryear, to breathe life back into those once-captive emotions.

As my long- and short-term memories fuse into a melodic counterpoint, the past melding with the present, my hope is to sweep aside the sticks and stones of embedded impedimenta and to finally root out the inauthentic, so that I may leave an unstained house for my children and grandchildren. To disentangle the self from the non-self, and to hold it up to the unflinching light of day is, I believe, as integral to my well being as the earth I walk, the air I breathe and the sun that stills my unsure heart.

Couldn't She Find an Englishman?

Darling, do your remember…?
Touch me, remind me who I am.

Stanley Kunitz

It had been four years since we had slept a quiet sleep or lived an ordinary day, and London was being bombed almost continuously. War-weary, our cupboards bare, we awaited Armageddon with pounding hearts, along with an unshakable belief in the righteousness of our mission.

I was working as a secretary at the American Embassy when Art arrived at the end of October 1943. A civilian physicist sent to London by the U.S. Navy Department, Art was to consult with the British about anti-submarine warfare.
A mutual friend had suggested that we might like each other, so our meeting that rainy day was not without expectations.

Traveling on military air transport planes for three days, Art arrived looking bedraggled, exhausted, and somewhat sinister. He wore a black trench coat and a wide-brimmed hat many sizes too large, and as he removed his hat and shook off the rain, I took in his sallow complexion, dark auburn hair, and restless brown eyes. *Oh my God,* I thought, *He looks like Al Capone.* Unnerved and sensing a sort of wariness between us, I plunged ahead with pleasantries. I hoped his trip had been uneventful, his hotel comfortable, had his luggage arrived all right?

Not once did he look at me as we spoke, so I assumed my face had shattered any optimism he might have indulged. My romantic fantasies evaporated along with our conversation. Art asked a few desultory questions about his fellow team members, thanked me, and with an audible sense of relief we said goodbye. Watching him depart for his hotel, my heart whispered, *You will marry this man.* My head shot back, *Not on your life.* But my heart was silent.

The next day Art wandered back into my office and suggested that we lunch together. "There seems to be no one else around," he added. It was the most backhanded invitation I had ever accepted. With the usual lunchtime air raid in progress, we darted into a crowded pub on Oxford Street close to Marble Arch. As we made sporadic conversation, Art again avoided looking directly at me and focused instead on the trendy occupants of a nearby table. I made a vow never again to date this disquieting American.

Despite our uneasy encounters, and my declared vow of exclusion, Art and I drifted towards one another, moved by an instinct that neither of us questioned. And soon I found myself sharing yet another lunch and then dinners with him. Since Art knew little of small talk, I recall my endless chattering that sometimes evolved into monologue, in my endeavor to appease those fearful, empty places inside of me. Eventually, though, I found my way out of this dilemma by asking Art one fixating question: *"What is Physics?"* His answer, sparkling with enthusiasm, continued unabated for fifty-two years. No longer living in the shadow of Al Capone, I began to hear the music in Art's voice and caught the warmth in his eyes when he chanced to look at me.

* * *

As the holidays approached, I invited Art to spend Christmas with me in Kent, to meet my oldest friends, Peg and Laurence. The annual Christmas Eve party at the embassy began to gear up around mid-morning. By the time Art arrived, I was happily numbed. Hearing his easy laugh from across the room, I watched him greet friends, looking relaxed and fuzzy-warm in his tweed overcoat with his red muffler hugging his neck. My usual restraint loosened, I charged over to welcome him, almost knocking him down with a kiss. Our first. Resting against Art I felt attached to him like a limpet to its rock and wanted to stay in that safe place forever.

We were still holding on to one another an hour later as we left the party by taxi for Victoria Station. Crowded with servicemen and -women and civilians intent on getting home for the holiday, the fortress-like station simmered with anticipation. As the excitement of the jostling crowd merged into my own unsteady state, I inexplicably tossed my handbag and my large bouquet of yellow chrysanthemums into the air. Art carefully picked up each flower and the contents of my bag—no easy feat in the gloom of the enforced blackout—and neither of us said a word. I was hiding my embarrassment behind an acquired nonchalance and feeling queasy from all that unaccustomed champagne.

On the train we shared a compartment with a shy British soldier who was about to see his family after two years on active duty. After we'd exchanged a few niceties, I felt my stomach perform an abrupt about-turn. I struggled to move out of societal range, but I was no match for upcoming events, and vomited a direct hit onto his immaculate uniform. That valiant young man took it in stride. He even apologized with true British stolidness for any inconvenience he might have caused, as Art and I endeavored to clean him up. Now, decades later, my memory scans every nuance of that scene, the chugging train, my unsteady self, Art's unhesitating support… and I hold an enduring tenderness toward that unknown soldier, wherever he might be.

It was close to midnight when we arrived in Kent. In the blackout, we felt our way off the train; I knew we had to climb a steep hill, and at the top we would find Peg and Laurence's cottage. Art trudged up, carrying our suitcases and my flowers—and to a certain extent me. Peg opened the door and I said, "This is Art." Then I passed out.

* * *

125

Back in London, we went to the ballet together, to the theater, to parties. And when the Underground shut down during heavy air raids, we shared virginal nights in Art's flat in Chelsea. Life in wartime London was exhilarating. In the face of evil we countered the chaos surrounding us with a righteous defiance and an unending supply of adrenaline. Along with everyone else, we forgot how to feel tired.

A few weeks after Christmas, Art and I were on the sofa-bed in his living room, warmed by a glowing coal fire and holding each other against the unquiet night. "I have something to say," he looked at me, his voice hesitant, lacking its usual vibrancy. My immediate thought was that he was returning to the States, or worse that there was someone already in his life and he was ending our relationship. Uncharacteristically, I remained silent. "I want you to marry me." He continued, "Would you?" I felt a rush of relief and joy and then just as suddenly fear and desolation moved in, as if I'd opened a window onto a frozen, uninhabitable landscape. Lacking the courage to utter the unequivocal, "Yes," I replied by asking, "When?"

With the air raids over London intensifying, we decided to marry in a village southeast of the city. Early on the morning of March 24th we boarded the train to Claygate. As we walked up the lane to the church, I began to think about a future in a new country with a man about whom I knew relatively little. Was it love I felt for Art, or was I merely flirting with the concept of love? Art must have sensed my anxiety, because halfway to the church he stopped and turned to hug me. In that wordless interlude, I began to learn about trust.

My father had chosen not to appear at my wedding, explaining with tears in his voice that he did not wish to upset my mother, so my mother's father had reluctantly agreed to give me away. A detached, obdurate man, his only comment when he heard I was to marry Art had been, *"Couldn't she find an Englishman?"* Inside that small church, I recognized two people sitting on opposite sides of the aisle whose mutual loathing had stoked the every-week-a-new-disaster-story of my childhood: my mother to the right and my father's mother, whom I hadn't seen for more than a decade, to the left.

Walking down the aisle towards Art, I started to shake and was momentarily immobilized by the malevolent looks my mother and grandmother were shooting at each other. Dark memories invaded the church of a grandmother who'd always hated me, since I was my mother's daughter; a grandmother who was standing-in for her son, who had lacked the courage to face the woman whom he'd abandoned. So this is payback time, I remember thinking, with rising anger against my errant father who was exquisitely aware that the calculated appearance of his mother would likely trigger my mother into uncontrollable hysteria. When I finally reached Art—who knew nothing of the erupting passions—he simply took my hand and brought me back into the moment.

Back in London, ours was an unusual wedding night. Art came down with the flu and we had to spend the entire night in a shelter huddled with a group of strangers. The next morning we emerged, side by side, into the disorienting daylight. On the corner opposite our shelter stood four fire-watchers, drinking mugs of hot tea as the streets eased back to life and people went matter-of-factly about their business. The smell of burning pervaded the air around us as we walked toward Chelsea. We could see columns of smoke rising by the Thames a couple of blocks west. With my hand in Art's, the fearfulness of the night faded like a dream, leaving only the promise of meeting a new day and the beginning of our life together.

* * *

There was an especially heavy air raid as we departed by train three months later for Liverpool, where we were to embark on the *Mauritania* for New York City. On the dock where we waited, soldiers about to return to active duty were embracing their wives and children while lovers gave one another their farewells. Standing next to Art I felt a guilty comfort. Together we were moving into a world that knew no active war, while others were being pulled apart with the unthinkable thought that this might be their final embrace.

On the *Mauritania* there were only two other civilian couples. The rest of the passengers were military, including about five thousand German prisoners of war, many of them teenage boys en route to detention camps in the United States and Canada. Watching these boys swab the decks, I felt a terrible sadness, as if I were peering into the intimacy of another's distress. "Let's walk the other way," I said, turning to Art, and noticed that his eyes were also tearing as he moved us out of view. Later, we would learn that a German submarine had been tracking our ship across the Atlantic.

We arrived in Art's country—overwhelming to me in so many ways—stunning in its abundance, unsettling in its offers of instant friendship, so different from the painful reserve of the British. How could strangers be so accepting, I wondered. Art listened to my uncertainties and reassured me: *Take it easy. It will pass. Things change.*

My life with Art was not without its challenges. In many ways we were two people, miles apart at opposite ends of a spectrum, unconsciously searching for a balance to our lives. Such togetherness did not come without its dark moments as I had to learn a new system of ethics in my relationship with Art. Never before had I been offered such a guileless, trusting love which, by its very nature, assumed the reciprocity of a like response. No longer could I play my old game of chess, watching my opponent and calculating my responses. I had to peel away my old protective wrappings, expose myself to the light, wait fearfully for the negative to be printed and meet myself. And then what?

* * *

In 1951 we moved to Berkeley, California, back to the University of Art's graduate days, and where he was returning now to teach. We'd had our two children, Jonathan and Jennifer, and we settled into a lively community. I lived a happiness I'd never known. And then I broke apart.

The year I turned forty, each day turned into a battleground, where I feared my every step would meet a waiting land mine. I woke up shaking, my insides churning. If I ran into an acquaintance at the grocery store, I prayed for my hands not to quiver and for my face to remember its smile. Outwardly I faked my assured self: the cheerful mother, active in my children's schools, ever the supportive wife. Inwardly, though, an army was systematically tearing down the walls behind which I'd always hidden. At night, I was too afraid to drift into sleep. Terror lurked even in my dreams. Art was, as always, unflappable and resolute, but his assurances that my troubles would pass no longer worked. I managed to get myself to a therapist, and it was here a new journey of self-discovery began.

* * *

Coming from such different lifestyles, Art and I often brushed up against each other's idiosyncrasies. Art had to learn to deal with my need to connect with people—he considered my efforts to be overly-zealous—and I had to learn to understand his attitude toward others, which at times appeared downright dismissive. While Art's insecurities drove him away from people, mine sent me scurrying in their direction. I don't think I ever truly accepted that part of him, and it was the cause of our first quarrel.

We were living in Maryland during the first year of our marriage. I'd invited our neighbor, Karla, a concert pianist, to dinner. Over beef stroganoff, Karla plunged into talking (*even on the in-breath,* Art protested later) with the seductive aplomb of a seasoned monologist. As midnight approached and she began, yet again, a sentence with: "You know what?" Art replied, "I know what. It's time for you to go home." Karla found this remarkably amusing. I, however, did not. Arguing my case well into early morning, I got nowhere. I can still hear Art's gentle and bewildered voice in its non-comprehension, and my own clipped and accusatory tone: "How can you be so hurtful? One is never, rude to a guest." I lapsed into a punishing silence that I knew would devastate Art.

Over the years, we developed a modus vivendi that encompassed a certain gentle latitude toward each other's particularities. Like an oft-read script, we embraced our roles, neither of us wanting to disturb the equanimity of our life together, and neither of us admitting to the discontent of anger.

Throughout the 1950s and 1960s, the Physics Department at UC Berkeley was a close-knit group. We gathered together at each other's homes, where it was not unusual to find physicists and students discussing physics in one corner, with wives and girlfriends discussing their own spellbinding interests in the other. These were happy events for Art, events where he felt at ease, especially in our own home. At more intimate dinners, while I set out to please our hosts, Art would find the nearest bookcase or amuse the host's children or, better still, gravitate to the household pets. At houses where he knew few people, though, he'd wander around, with a glass in hand, waiting for release. Later he'd lament that as soon as he joined a group, they seemed to melt away in all directions.

People who knew Art delighted in his warmth, his sense of humor, his lively mind. Others found him hard to reach. An acquaintance of mine, who was seated next to Art at a dinner, confessed to me later that she had sensed his disapproval, since after his few desultory remarks, she was quietly ignored. I reassured her that, of course Art liked her—though sometimes I lied. Then there were times we'd find ourselves with people I knew Art didn't particularly like, and I'd watch him employ his first line of defense by contradicting their every utterance. I can still hear my pre-event plaintive, "Be nice." I can still hear Art's heartfelt reply, "But honey, I'm always nice." I'd push a little and Art would protest, "You want me to be more like you." Looking back, I see he had a point.

* * *

Now, over fifty years later, reflecting on the strivings we embrace in this joining with another, I realize it is an enterprise of heroic proportion, one devised by the gods (who themselves were not distinguished for their conjugal harmony) to challenge humankind. Perhaps we should be grateful to those trickster gods who push us to meet our truest self and to share that self with another. For each time we venture, it is gold in our basement.

Through the years, as Art and I changed so did our physical loving. A slower pace brought with it a deepening intimacy and the abiding comfort of awakening each morning to embrace one another's warm body. To the outward eye my aging body told my story, but to my inner eye the design seemed ageless and, instinctively, I still related to Art as that person I had met over fifty years ago. I wonder if all older people relate to the youth within the other, if this is how we protect ourselves from the knowledge of our mortality?

Ultimately, I would lose my protection. One evening in the winter of 1995, some ten years after Art was diagnosed with prostate cancer, we sat drinking wine before dinner and I left the table to turn on the oven. There are no walls between our dining room and kitchen, so I was able to see Art as he watched the garden settle down for the night. He appeared deep in thought. Then, as if continuing a conversation, he wept, "But I can never leave you." I returned to the table and held him and told him that he never would. Then we did what we always did when faced with the progression of his cancer: we filed the incident in our "pending" file. Art died of a cerebral hemorrhage three weeks later.

* * *

About a hundred people gathered in our home for Art's memorial. *One of the great experimental solid-state physicists, he was immune to the temptations of intellectual aggressiveness… always gentle, perceptive, modest, sympathetic and friendly* his obituary read. No sainthood was bestowed that afternoon in December, no long speeches, only warm vignettes of a man who had never ceased to be inspired by the beauty of the earth's formations. We ended that day by dancing to Fats Waller's "Your Feet's too Big," one of the songs Art used to sing to me when we lived in London, his voice sonorous, though a bit out of tune.

These days, without Art, it is I who retrieve the scattered pieces of my heart. Pick them up one by one and reassemble them as Art had once picked up those yellow chrysanthemums for me, long ago on that Christmas Eve at Victoria Station.

Elegy on Marriage

...a good marriage is that in which
each appoints the other guardian
of his solitude...

Rainer Maria Rilke

Tonight, tidying up my desk—the desk Art built for me—I chance upon a large manila envelope tucked under a pile of folders. Marked in Art's handwriting, *Letters: Joan to Art,* I feel that familiar aching jolt for when he was here, downstairs working or relaxing on the bed.

I sit up past midnight, reading the letters I'd written to him in 1945, during WWII when he was sent by the U.S. Navy Department to the Pacific. Memory is capricious, like an unreliable lover. Had Art simply read these letters to me, I'd have thought he was chatting up stories of his own making, the way he later delighted the children. But here they are, some in my own script, many typewritten—and oh, how breathlessly young, how blissfully adoring I sound. I was twenty-seven, Art, thirty-four.

I need to re-read these letters to remember who I was. These days, the future beckons the past and I, too, will soon leave—such is the order of things. As I dwell upon the life we shared for over fifty years, there is within a nagging imperative to dust around the edges, to leave a clean house.

High on an overdose of nostalgia, I study these flimsy, yellowed missives with the guilty fascination of the forbidden, as if I'm peering into the intimacies of strangers. The pleading, timorous, waif-like voice I hear does not belong to me. A blithe spirit, who weathered the Blitz in wartime London and treated the bombs with casual disrespect, I courted no one. Or so I thought. Yet, sixty-five years later, this letter tells our story:

> *May 1, 1945 ... I think so much about the kind of person I would have been without you and could love you alone for making me the kind of person I think I am, or am going to be. I'm sleepy sweetheart and want you just to kiss me goodnight. It's just the coldest thing in the world to be alone. I am resolved to have squads of children so that I can see you in all of them. Yes, I too, love you more than ever—if it's possible. I'm never going to do anything without you again— ever. Life is so beastly short, isn't it? And there is so much we have to do. All my love to my darling— Please come home soon. I'm just so alone without you. I can't imagine life without you now—I hope I die when you do.*

But it didn't work out that way. After Art died in 1995, my hopes were fixed upon living rather than dying. Beset by a lacerating grief, I'd awaken and howl my despair, then briskly forge ahead. Evenings, a warm breeze would touch my shoulders and, filled with an unexpected bliss, I'd dance around the house, my grief momentarily retreating. For months I lived a schizophrenic existence, interweaving the dark with the light while ignoring the echo of a voice that whispered, "Now you are free,"—the widow's syndrome that is oft-times heard, but rarely spoken. It was a voice that was to haunt me along with its companion, guilt.

Five years into widowhood, emboldened by my newfound independence, I wrote an essay titled *A Different Woman*. In it I questioned a few widowed friends about the freedom in their marriages. Did they yearn for their husbands to return Lazarus-like from the dead? While their answers reflected a certain ambivalence, I knew it was myself I was questioning. "Yes," I wrote, "I wanted Art back, every second of every hour, but it would be different." It would take another decade for me to clarify exactly what I meant by different.

* * *

How to replay a history of marriage? How to be objective in this sensitive, so tender a subject? Today, I walk a lonely walk, ever mindful of the quicksand beneath my feet and lament that Art isn't around to counter my monologue.

Here at my desk, the room assumes the ambience of a confessional. Writing is no longer a pleasure but is akin to pulling thorns out of reluctant flesh, and I am held within a great sadness unlike any I can remember. Instinctively, I reach for letters I've written to Art in the timelessness of his reality. The present dissolves into the past.

> *August 16, 2010 ... Dearest Darling. Tell me where I belong. Age and atrophy are insinuating bedfellows. I'm watching parts of myself disappear and sense that any moment I shall close my eyes and float away into the receiving ether. My aim is to be graceful in this unplanned journey. But habits run deep ruts. Age and energy conspire to ground my thinking. Too often I lack the wisdom of acceptance and yearn for younger days, when I dwelt within the known landscape. I think of you as your strength waned—days when you could no longer sprint up our front steps; the quiet way in which you coped after your first stroke; your re-mastering of speech and of the computer—all of which you did with unfailing grace. I used to think you were hiding from reality. In hindsight, though, I realize*

that was my stuff, not yours, since you recognized
change as an inevitable part of the ordered life.

* * *

Art would be exactly one hundred years old today and I wonder why I'm still plagued by that initial whispered insinuation, "Now you are free." Through the years, that voice, which I resolutely disregarded, has become increasingly strident as if to compel debate. At my age time no longer dances a slow waltz, and I am reluctantly pushed to ask, "Free from *what?*"

My answer may be as convoluted as the question is simplistic, since I can think of no unprintable truth, no unforgivable episode that bedeviled our marriage and left me praying for widowhood. Art was the dearest of men, who became my steadfast enabler. He was also at times obstinate, judgmental, and given to excessive punditry. I, on the other hand, was critical, controlling, and at times lacking in compassion. We were both gloriously and painfully human.

Toward the end of Art's life, the tenor of my days shifted from its familiar congeniality to a nagging discontent. I felt trapped in a system not of my choosing as waves of resentment and anger drifted in and out like a discordant melody. Art, meanwhile, happily ensconced in his daily routine, appeared oblivious of my anger that persisted like a rallying cry to arms. Somewhere in the dark underworld of my psyche a rebellion was brewing and for a while my perfect marriage felt less than idyllic. There was one night in the aloneness of our bed, when Art, more tired than usual, wanted me there with him to hug him into sleep. Through the years, our togetherness in bed had always been our comfort zone. We'd listen to music, make love, make amends. But on that night, sunk in my nearby chair, I ignored his entreaties and continued to read, immersed in a broody, confused withdrawal. If Art noticed my disquiet, he didn't comment. Uniformly complicit in our hesitancy to disturb the undertow of our collective psyches, we carefully avoided subjects that would ruffle the calm we clung to.

In many ways, an aging marriage is kin to an aging house. Things shift. Cracks appear. If left unattended, dry rot creeps in and frays the foundation. Built upon the shifting sands of chance, the institution of marriage is a miracle to contemplate. We love, cherish and, in my archaic generation, promise to obey. But in fact we are all strangers, bearing ancestral templates to a beloved. It may take a life time for many of us to disengage from who we are not, to who we are. Strangers to ourselves, how can we really know another?

I realize now that Art and I were both stuck in appeasing the dragons of our childhood. In Art's family, anger was an ungodly flaw, an emotion that was never addressed. In my family, anger was an emotion that thrived on endless repetition; the antidote to my mother's breaking heart and an everyday pollutant I prayed to avoid. It was rare that Art and I quarreled. But should I argue my point too strongly on a contentious issue, he would sharply and firmly end the discussion. Ironically, in our efforts to avoid anger, we unwittingly deprived ourselves of that singular intimacy that is born out of conflict, pierces the veneer of conjugal comfort and enlivens.

Writing about the intimate unfolding of my marriage is a delicate subject that leaves me feeling naked in the company of strangers, and terribly alone. I've been dancing around that lingering question, "Free from *what?*" and have spent enumerable hours writing soulful scenarios of Art's inadequacies. My catchy solution, "Why isn't a man more like a woman?" leads nowhere. My stomach tightens into its hard knot, when I hedge a truth since these were hollow meanderings and I knew it. Then I hear Art's voice, somewhat testily, telling me to get to the point.

My point is that the prophetic whisper, "Now you are free" had it exactly right. The act of writing divorces fact from fiction, and gradually I have learned that within the unthinkable grief of widowhood there floats a renascent freedom that has nothing to do with my love for Art. It is a subtle freedom that goes to the core of a woman's emancipation from her age-long role of societal subservience. I think of it as the space wherein lie the jewels of a woman's femininity. My role is to reclaim these intuitive, jeweled parts, to incubate them into a holy awareness that tells me who I am. That tells me freedom is not given or taken but is within.

* * *

In my revisiting eye, I watch now as Art and I dance our initial pas de deux, swing into our impassioned tango, gentle into our amicability, and ache within our dissonances. But too soon the dance is over, leaving only the requiem.

Then I remember that other place, the place where Art is always around. We're sitting in our usual chairs, drinking tea at our dining room table. We meet each other through the prism of our original observing eye, with its inerasable ardency, back when we were young and lithe. Art asks how things go, and I tell him," Oh, okay, though I'm not quite ready to finish this essay. Writing about us keeps us close and, besides, there's always the pain in the pit of my stomach each time I finish a piece." We caress hands with that tender wonder of the new mother, and I feel the familiar, easy contentment of our yesteryears.

I ask Art what he's been doing and he laughs his vibrant laugh and says, "Nothing much," in a tone I so well recognize. Times past, he'd come home for dinner, before rushing back to his lab to verify the day's success of a long-confounding physics experiment, and I'd get the same answer to my eager question. Another reason, I tell myself, that quiet men choose chatty wives. Art asks what's rumbling my mind. "The past," I reply, "is rumbling." He tells me my essay is a bit long -winded, though parts of it make him weep. I don't ask which parts. I'm thinking that marriage is a golden chalice into which we pour our being: who we are, who we are not; who we yearn to become. "I'd like a second chance, a redemptive re-run." I say. He settles back, looks into my unquiet eyes and smiles.

Watching Myself Disappear

All the world's a stage,
And all the men and women merely players.

William Shakespeare

"Promise you'll ask Aunt Joan to write me a letter to tell me she's really, really not afraid of becoming bones." Kip, my great nephew, had spent the afternoon at a friend's house. Walking home holding his mother's hand, his natural ebullience disappeared into a chasm of gloom as he wondered with increasing bewilderment, what it felt like to *become* bones. It turns out, he and his friend had been looking at pictures of mummies, skeletons tucked into catacombs, and the imagination of a five year old took its first step into questioning one of life's imponderables. After my conversation with Brooke, Kip's mother, I wrote the following letter.

> *Dear Kip,*
>
> *I hear that you looked at some pictures of mummies and got to wondering what it would be like to "become bones." And then, you thought about me, whose bones are especially ancient. I love that your thoughts drift across 3,000 miles from your house in Connecticut to my house in California. You ask if I'm afraid of becoming bones—if I am scared. That's an important question. My answer is No. Each age is a*

new adventure, isn't it? The only difference is that you know where you are going—like, one of these days, into first grade—whereas I don't know. I can only dream about where I'm going. And this makes it more exciting. Write me again if you have more questions, since I love questions and I love you.
—Aunt Joan

This seemed to have settled the matter for Kip, but it hasn't for me. It is the word "exciting" that resonates with a glibness that rankles my insomniac critic. Did I choose this word merely to protect the sensibilities of a five-year old? Am I truly sanguine about my imminent adventure, or have I built a moat of deception around an unbearable fear of immigrating into unchartered territory?

I watch the questions of my wandering mind with distinct unease and wish I hadn't asked them. Upon reflection, my questions do hold a certain authenticity in that my equilibrium depends entirely on a continuing symbiosis with my lifelong, well-defined rut, as any change, especially of location, is anathema to my being. My doctor, who has been my rock for over thirty-five years, moves his practice from Berkeley to nearby Oakland, an area I know well. I panic. On my way to his new location, I pass his old office and feel orphaned and teary as if that three-story brick building, whose parking attendant greets me with fatherly familiarity, has disowned me.

One month later, I sit facing my computer screen with a mind empty of inspiration and a subject matter that refuses to cooperate. And since I am the subject, there is no other I can beguile to gloss over an impending sense of entrapment. Unlike Houdini, I have no escape route. No more death defying acts. Watching myself disappear is my final offering. And while the theme may intrigue, confound, and possibly irritate a reader, I, the writer, am seized with waves of helplessness and a drifting incompetence. Words no longer shimmer like sunlight on raindrops, but demand excavation from deep within, while fear intones that my ability to write is fading, along with my brain cells. Then I remember that fear also carries a message, so I calm down, tune in, and wait. Eventually, in the middle of the night when my conscious mind is less guarded, I hear, "Which self are you talking about, Joan?"

This is not the consolatory message I've hoped for. No soothing of my fears, no discourse on the brilliance of my brain cells. Only a Socratic inspired dialogue that nudges to explore the who of me. When I stop to ask myself why this recalcitrant essay seems to have no idea where it's going, the answer shoots back: "So, do you know where *you're* going?"

* * *

This morning, in the kitchen before breakfast, I am greeted by a colony of uninvited worker ants, swarming over counters and into the honey container, into bowls of sugared almonds, raisins, leftover apple slices, snacks I leave around to keep me standing when my energy sinks to zero. Reluctant to inflict pain on any living thing—though the options are few and, anyway, I'm pissed—I unhesitatingly drown every collectible ant in the sink. Later, washing dishes, I look onto the garden flattened into submissive humility by the last torrential rainstorm that flooded the Bay Area. Then the sun returns, and the garden rises to greet it, while the crows and blue jays fight for primacy of the birdfeeder. My neighbor's cat checks out the birds, while the ever-vigilant squirrel in the Mallow tree checks out the cat. This familiar picture of nature in progress leads me to fantasize about the inhabitants of the garden, of the foraging house-hold ants, of my neighbor's black cat and animals in general. Do they have a visceral sense of their endings and beginnings?

While we human animals are cognizant of endings, with our diverse themes and variations, I wonder to what extent we are aware of beginnings? I'm not thinking of that original thrust out of a garden of plentitude into an awaiting landscape where we must cry in order to live. How aware are we of our first moments on this earth, when blurred sight and awakening senses gradually evolve into a self?

And then, once again, my mind echoes that middle-of-the-night unsettling question, "Which self are you talking about, Joan?" It is a question I think about unceasingly, but nothing definitive rises to mind, only hesitant replies that lack conviction. In despair at an immovable impasse, I decide that thinking leads nowhere. I decide that my allotted time span is not waiting for me to catch up, that surely there is a more dexterous route. So I relax into a few deep breaths and wait. By some sleight of hand, channels switch, the impasse lifts, time reverses itself, and I am viewing images, once again, from long ago.

* * *

World War I, London, 1917. I am three months old. Sirens warn of the approaching Graff Zeppelin airship. My mother wraps my sister and me in a heavy eiderdown that scratches. She rushes us in our pram, bumping through the streets, across the square, into the bomb shelter of the local school. The shelter is filled with the elderly, exhausted mothers, frightened children. There are no fathers around. They are away, fighting in France. Over the years, my mother, with her familiar panache, repeats the bomb shelter story and with each repetition her narrative, by extension, becomes mine.

* * *

Uncle Len, my father's half-brother, who lives in the flat across the road, drops in for tea. He plops down at the opposite end of the sofa from where I am reading. My mother leaves the room to make tea and my uncle, who tells jokes I do not understand, stretches his legs out, across my lap. I'm unable to move. His legs press down on mine. I am mute with embarrassment. My mother returns with the tea and I hear, "Leonard, take your legs off that child." He laughs. He says that he didn't know they were on me, while I sit glued to the sofa, crimson with shame. That evening, I hear my mother inform my father that she will not allow Leonard to enter our flat again, that he should not be around an eleven year old. My father tells my mother that she is, as usual, exaggerating, I feel it's all my fault.

* * *

In the hall outside the head mistress' room, I stand waiting for my name to be called. Students look at me with pity. They identify with my terror as they rush to class. They, too, have faced the threat of the waiting guillotine. Thirteen years old, I am the class clown, which brings abiding admiration and loyalty from my peers. This morning, our room teacher, whom we all call "Chimp" arrived early and observed me mimicking her worst attributes. I am sent to the headmistress to await punishment. Once inside the room, though, I am ignored. Miss Morant continues to work at her desk. Finally she turns around and requests that I tell her in detail exactly why I am there. The punishment is handed out: I am barred from all sports activities for one month. This is a death sentence. I am sports captain of my class. Sports is the subject I excel in. It's thereason I stay in school.

* * *

I dream of these vignettes over and over, and sense they hold the answer, however enigmatic, to the all-pervasive question of self. I watch the embattled ego manipulate my shaky world from way back then, and recognize these selves today, ever alert, nestled among my family of infinite selves. The self I'm talking about is not a single entity but a conglomeration of selves shaped by events, and refined into an evolving masterpiece that is never finished.

* * *

This morning I'm propelled by an unceasing urge to clean house, a particular feminine attribute that invades at times of stress. Remember that pulsing pre-menstrual energy? As I relieve the refrigerator of its decaying leftovers and wash the grime off the kitchen floor, my thoughts drift within, to the implacable reality that hovers beneath the exigencies of old age. Increasingly, who I am today, is not who I was yesterday.

My son, Jon, whom I haven't seen for a couple of months, arrives today from Los Angeles, and I gear up to match his expectations. He reiterates how proud he is of a mother who copes as well as I, whose mind is unfailing and who seems impervious to change. And while, in the past, we've discussed more formal matters concerning my eventual demise, death as a consequence of life is, for him, a verboten subject. But time escapes, old evasions no longer work, and I am forced to acknowledge bodily imperfections. Our first morning at breakfast Jon remarks, "Your hand is shaking." I expect this, since I know his gimlet eye, his ready tongue. I also know his secreted heart of infinite tenderness. "Yes," I reply, looking into his eyes, "I shake in the mornings these days."

Partners for ninety-five years, my body and I share a symbiotic relationship with varying degrees of collegiality. We also share a binding love as we coexist within the house we call *myself*. At times, we politely ignore each other. Other times, we exchange unprintable invectives, and too often we unwittingly inflict mutual pain. The affair between body and self requires a delicate balance, since divorce is out of the question. There are no rules, only drifting waves of conciliation that move us together and pull us apart.

A demanding partner in my youth, I yearned to become a prima ballerina, and practiced on my toes too soon and too long, such that my legs bowed out, requiring repair and rest. In my teens, my heart murmured with exhaustion from excessive athletic workouts at school, and I was sentenced to six months of complete rest. And always there was the gut that rebelled against the chronic stress in my household. My body was an unequal partner back then, a silent appendage to my conflicted desires. In old age, the body speaks more vociferously. It directs the traffic. It observes all systems as they prepare for final take off.

Sunday at noon, I sit in my chair in the garden as the sun massages my weary bones, and watch the hummingbirds zoom into the seduction of the red-tipped salvia bush. I, however, am not zooming. For the past few weeks my energy has barely risen above zero. My heart has episodes of fibrillation, my gut intolerant of its surroundings. Stray thoughts flutter my unease. I recall a conversation with a longtime friend who once remarked that I never change, that I look the same now as I did fifty years ago. My scripted rejoinder, with a slight shrug, simply "One never knows. Overnight I might turn into a wizened old woman." And my mind murmurs, *Perhaps the future is now.* Shivering a little, I move into that soft, still space between each breath, where there is no Thought and where fear is unknown.

My daughter, Jennifer, is visiting from Guatemala and I am pampered, perhaps too much. She delights in this reversal of roles. Walking in the park, she takes my hand to steady my gait. She drives my car, cavalier fashion, the way I do. She shops and cooks with the aplomb of an exuberant Julia Child. In short, she is a fussy, indulgent mother. She gardens and fills the house with roses, plays music, burns incense and enlivens a house that's sobered down, along with its occupant. Meanwhile, I drift into the role of the receiving one, with its allure and its inherent dangers. It is a fine line between the easy pleasure of acceptance, the concomitant fear of dependence and the unthinkable loss of control. I'm stunned to realize the many years of unremitting struggle I've spent to control my life on this earth. It is as though I've lived in a perpetual war zone with my finger on the Alert button. To lose control, is by definition to lose the self. Now, as I fade into my leaving, I observe my infinite selves navigating a path in an unpredictable world. I sense the presence of an irreplaceable love, linked with the weightlessness of an indwelling paradise.

For the past weeks, I've been haunted by a writer's ultimate fear: how to get from here to there? In my mind the landscape is crystal clear, but as I follow its path I arrive at an abyss of nothingness. I try other paths, as if to circumvent an enemy, but they lead to the reverberating silence of a void. Panic moves in. I fantasize that perchance I've been dealt a relentless Sisyphean task as atonement for mortal sins, or most devastating, that my brain is on permanent vacation, nevermore to delight or frustrate with its mischief. I sit back in my computer chair, look up through the skylight as the late sun flickers through the overhanging bay trees and an eerie thought jolts my thinking: I am not writing this essay. This essay is writing me.

* * *

Sunday afternoon, Justine arrives for tea. A native New Englander, endowed with firm convictions and unwavering integrity, we met in Berkeley in the 50's and our friendship endures through the dark and the light of our years. Six months since we've been together, we catch up on our families, note the inevitability of our faltering bodies—a subject the elderly invariably decide they will not address, but always do—then quickly move to more lively subjects. Woman to woman connections are a singular delight and a wellspring of comfort in our fast-paced era, where intimacy is less frequently shared across the table, but rendered in sound bites across the miles. Too soon, time evaporates and Justine, who no longer drives, reaches for her cell phone to call a cab. Meanwhile, for the past half hour, I am ignoring an inner turbulence that echoes the trembling of an approaching earthquake. The magnet deep within that controls every one of my body parts, has slipped off kilter. All parts of me are gliding into outer space. My center is falling apart. My center no longer holds.

* * *

"I think I'm having a stroke," I say to the man at the desk. I am instructed to sign in and wait. I obediently take a seat next to Justine, whose cab I shared to Alta Bates Emergency Room. I tell Justine that she doesn't have to wait, that she should go home. "I have no intention of leaving," Justine answers in her no-nonsense way. Soon I am moved to an examination room, where oxygen is administered, my heart monitored. A comforting liquid drips into my arm. In a medicated glow, I am thinking that I ought not be here, that maybe I've made the whole thing up, that perhaps it's only my aging mind that has slipped. Justine continues to sit in the quiet with me. Three hours later, I am moved upstairs to the 6th floor stroke unit. Justine puts my belongings into a locker and leaves. I am alone in a two-bed room with a glittering view and a team of remarkable nurses.

* * *

Back home, three days later, I gaze at the enduring redwood trees in the park across the street and think about the gauntlet that has been thrown at my feet; the perennial battle between persona and self. Family and friends congratulate me on my glowing appearance, but my thoughts remind me that this is my second stroke in as many years. "Three strikes and you are out," an adage from my childhood, clearly applies. My future is shrouded in uncertainty; Death, the irrefutable certainty.

* * *

Upstairs in my room, I sit and look out the window. Down on the street, hanging on the rearview mirror of my Honda

Accord, I glimpse the familiar blue sign that defines the driver as disabled. I contemplate the wheelchair logo with resigned acceptance and a hint of shame that suggests demotion to a lesser rank. The flow of my life now depends upon others. I fear I may never drive again, never grocery shop alone, never dwell in blessed solitude. I'm painfully aware of a time delay between my mind's desire and my brain's reaction. My short-term memory lingers for a bare millisecond, to be just as quickly forgotten. *Did I take that elongated white capsule or didn't I?* The tutored, positive self disappears into a chasm of bewilderment, while every demon of doubt stealthily invades my territory. My familiar, confident rhetoric no longer holds. Each day, I watch myself fade like the final rays of a setting sun. And all the while, underlying a known reality, I am being bathed in an ocean of inexpressible bliss, an amorphous energy, that is everywhere and which I sense will never leave.

I'd hoped to end with more answers than questions, more poetry than prose. However, unlike Icarus, I'm aware that my aim is too high. What keeps me up at night is how to describe the beauty, pain, unbelievable opportunity, compassion and unfathomable love of this world as I've come to know it. There is a sense of continuity in being here while at the same time disappearing into that which we are all a part of. Very soon I will leave the known and travel to the unknown. As it turns out, my final words aren't so complicated a thing to say after all, dear reader. It's not about the head…it's about the heart. The heart is what forever leads the way.